CW01394770

Don't Let It Get You Down Syndrome

S.K.Dinning

First published 2014. Revised 2017.

Copyright © S.K.Dinning 2014

The right of S.K.Dinning to be identified as the author of this book has been asserted in accordance with Section 77 and 78 of the Copyrights, Designs and Patents Act 1988. Copying of this manuscript, in whole or in part, without the written permission of the author or his publisher is strictly prohibited and would constitute a breach of copyright held.

To contact the author please visit www.skdinning.co.uk

Contents

Chapter 1: The Body in the Library

I don't know why I kept thinking it would be a good idea to take Jamie to the library. We went there many times when he was young, and it never went well. But, like Charlie Brown running up to kick the football, saying to himself "This is the time that I will finally get to kick it!" I said to myself "This is the time we will finally have a nice father-son bonding session over some lovely picture books, and it won't end in frustration and/or humiliation." But I was always wrong. Jamie always pulled that metaphorical football away.

The first time I ever took him, he was a toddler, in his pushchair. I was sure he would love it at the library, because he loved books and bedtime stories, and surely the sight of shelves full of books would bring a smile to his little face? I wheeled him through the sliding doors, and turned the pushchair around to see his expression when he saw all the books. When I saw his face, it was not the reaction I was expecting - he did not look happy. In fact, he looked a little nauseous. He started to retch, and I quickly reached out just as he threw up, and I caught it perfectly in my cupped hands. Now, I don't know if you have ever found yourself in a public library with both hands full of warm baby sick and four librarians staring at you in a concerned manner, but let me tell you it is not a pleasant experience. I had no idea what to do, but as the vomit began to seep through my fingers, I knew that I had to do it quickly.

Over the next few years, despite the unpromising start, we continued to go back again and again. Each time it was a disaster, but for different reasons. Sometimes Jamie would run around the library giggling, sometimes he would throw himself at other children and demand cuddles. One time we foolishly attempted a parent-toddler story time session, and Jamie kept snatching the book from the poor old lady who was trying to read *Commotion in the Ocean* to a small crowd of bemused toddlers and their irritated parents. One time we did not even make it into the library, because on the way Jamie unscrewed the lid from his milk bottle, and poured the contents down the front of my trousers.

But it was the last time I took him that really sticks in my mind. I say "the last time" and that is exactly what I mean. We can never go back.

Jamie and I arrived at the library in the middle of a busy Saturday afternoon. Holding Jamie's hand as I strode confidently through the doors, I smiled at the librarian behind the counter. I did not recognize her, but I assumed she remembered us; I think most people probably remember us. My intention was to pick up a few picture-books for Jamie and a couple of novels for Meg, but I thought it would be nice to show Jamie round the books and perhaps read a few stories to him first. I have no idea why I thought it would be a pleasant way to pass the time - clearly I had forgotten the previous dozen-or-so visits.

Nevertheless I was as optimistic as ever as I led Jamie towards the children's book section, where I tried to draw his attention to the picture books.

"Ooh look Jamie, it's *There's An Ouch in My Pouch* - we like that one don't we?

No Jamie, don't go over there, those books are for older children, you wouldn't like those.

What's that you've picked up?"

It was *Smith*, by Leon Garfield, and I was momentarily distracted by the memory of reading it myself at school and noticing that it seemed to be the same edition. That was the point at which Jamie decided to launch it across the library; it fluttered over my head and landed a few metres behind me with a soft thud. I span around quickly to pick it up, but that was a mistake; I should have restrained Jamie first, because while I was picking the book up I heard another fluttering sound followed by a soft thud, as *The Voyage of the Dawn Treader* landed nearby. I turned back to face Jamie, and narrowly avoided being hit in the face by *Stig of the Dump*. In the time it took me to reach him he also managed to launch a collection of

Aesop's Fables and a *Rainbow Fairies* novel. Flutter, Flutter. Thud! Thud!

Libraries are much friendlier places now than they used to be. The days when a stern-faced librarian would "shush" anyone who raised their voice above a whisper have long gone. Exactly what the modern etiquette is for libraries is a little vague, but I instinctively knew that parents who allowed their children to throw the books around the library would be frowned upon. I needed to take immediate action.

Jamie chuckled as I told him off and made him pick up all the books. Even though I was a little cross, I had to admire the fact that he had thrown the older children's books and not the toddlers' picture books – not because of the more mature subject matter, but because he had demonstrated that he had instinctively known that the small paperbacks were going to be more aerodynamic than the big books for pre-schoolers.

After another couple of failed attempts to interest Jamie in the picture books, I abandoned the idea and decided instead to focus on getting something for Meg.

I led Jamie by the hand over towards the *G* section of adult fiction, looking for a Philippa Gregory novel that Meg might not have read. She has a love of historical fiction and I knew she would be pleased if I could find something she had not come across before. As soon as we got near the shelves though, Jamie started trying to grab the books, so I had to restrain him by holding onto both hands. However, he then started trying to knock the books off the shelves with his feet, and I was finding it very difficult to stop him.

I should have given up and taken him home at that point, but I was determined to get Meg something to read, so I came up with a solution - I put him on my back. Jamie loves a piggy-back, so I was sure he would co-operate, and if he was behind me then he would not be able to reach the books, right? Well, yes and no. Because I stood far enough back from the books, Jamie could not reach them; however, I forgot about the shelf of books behind us. Jamie did not forget. My heart sank as I heard the sound of *Catch 22* flying across the room and landing in Philosophy and Psychology. I took half a step forward so that he could no longer reach the books behind him, and I hoped that he still could not reach the books in front of him. I saw his hands reach out, and sure enough, he could not quite reach the books - however, he could reach the shelf itself. What happened next seemed to happen in slow motion. I saw him grab the shelf in front of us with both hands, and I felt him tense up as he put his not inconsiderable strength into his grip. For a split second I though he was going to pull the whole shelf down, but then I felt his

9

body twist, as he used his knees to throw me off balance. My own knees buckled, and with Jamie's weight on my back I went down hard to the floor. Lying in a heap, I groaned. Several of my limbs were spread out at unnatural angles, and my body was crumpled and squashed in a way that made me worry for my internal organs.

What worried me most though, was the thought that Jamie must also have been hurt when we fell. Had I landed on top of him? Surely that would break a rib or two, or worse? Maybe an arm or a leg? What if he had banged his head when he fell? He was still on my back so I could not see him, but he had suddenly gone very quiet. After what was probably only a second or two, I felt him move again. He was okay! I was elated. I realised I could not be angry with him for knocking me down - I was just so relieved he was not seriously hurt that I felt no anger, just love. I felt him moving again.

Then I heard a familiar fluttering sound, followed by a distant soft thud, and a low chuckling in my ear.

Chapter 2: Down and Disorderly

Jamie has Down's syndrome. This won't come as a big surprise to you, given the clue in the title of the book, and the picture of the little fella on the front.

Jamie is also on the autistic spectrum. You might possibly find this news unexpected, since it is not immediately apparent from the front cover, but it is mentioned in the blurb on the back of the book, and in the description on Amazon, so unless you are one of those kamikaze readers who just looks at the cover then ploughs straight in, you probably already knew that too.

Jamie is also possessed by a malign entity – a mischievous spirit. I bet you never saw that one coming – it's not on the back of the book and I have asked reviewers not to mention it so as not to spoil the surprise. Yes, he is possessed by quite a famous nature sprite called Jack-o-Red, who was famous for his destructive impulses and his charm with the ladies. He was revered by the Celtic shamen in the dark ages, until he fell out with them over the dual issues of gay marriage and women druids.

Okay, I am kidding about the spirit possession. For a moment there you were thinking "Uh oh, it is one of *those* books." The bit about the Down's syndrome and the autism is true though. He also has ADHD, and I think he might have Tourette's Syndrome too, but so far no doctors have agreed with me.

I have raised Jamie with my lovely wife Meg for the past twelve years and it has not been easy. I would describe it as being somewhere between *The Curious Incident of the Dog in the Night Time* and *We Need to Talk About Kevin*. There cannot be many people in the position I was in while reading Mark Haddon's book, thinking "I will see your Autism and raise you a Down's syndrome." On the other hand though, I cannot really complain too much because Jamie has never gone on a killing spree.

Sometimes I tell people about Jamie's dual conditions and then watch their faces as they process the information. Most people don't know what to make of it. I see them wondering whether he fits the Down's syndrome stereotype (affectionate, fun loving, gentle) or the autistic one (anxious, distant, brilliant at counting cards in casinos). Surely he cannot be both, as they seem so different?

More often than not, after a few seconds deliberation, they ask the same question:

"Wherever did he get his ginger hair from?"

I don't know what it is about the slightly awkward social situation of being around a disabled child that makes people feel the need to lighten the mood by implying that Jamie's paternity is questionable, and that perhaps my wife has been a little free with her affections and that we are all in fact living a lie, but they do. Sometimes I see them mulling over the fact that my best friend at the time, Max, also had ginger hair, and wondering whether or not to mention it.

I am not worried of course. I know that both Meg and I have relatives with ginger hair, and I know that the only way Meg would ever have touched Max would have been to push him from a tall building. Nevertheless, it does seem to bother some people.

Down's syndrome is a genetic condition. A lot of people think that Down's syndrome is associated with missing chromosomes, but actually the opposite is true. People with Down's syndrome have an extra chromosome - they have inherited three copies of the genes on chromosome 21, rather than the usual two.

I am not going to pretend that I know what all that means. Many years ago I did once pretend - a genetics nurse came round to our house when Jamie was a baby, and explained it to us using diagrams and leaflets. She showed us a picture that was supposed to represent some chromosomes which looked as though someone had carefully sorted a handful of maggots and worms into similar sized pairs on the screen of a photocopier, before pressing the copy button.   I nodded along as she talked us through it, as though it all made sense to me, but it was all quite overwhelming really. What I did pick up, was that it was a condition Jamie had had since the first moment when the egg was fertilised. It affects every cell in his body – it is not a disease, and there is not a cure, and there never will be.

So why is it called "Down's syndrome" (or possibly "Down syndrome" depending on whether you live in the USA or the UK)? Some people have a vague idea that it is something to do with the word 'down' - a negative word - perhaps something to do with the person's appearance, or maybe his/her intelligence or disposition. Again, this is not the case. The condition is named after the doctor who first recognized the characteristics of the syndrome in 1866, Dr John Langdon Down.

If he had been called Dr Up, my son would now have a condition called "Up's syndrome", which is far more positive. It actually sounds to me like quite a cool thing to have. More appropriate too. I think new parents would be pleased to find out their child had Up's syndrome, and it would make those first few days far less traumatic. All the other kids in the neighbourhood would hear about the kid with Up's syndrome and be jealous.

"Mummy, why can't I have Up's syndrome like that kid next door?"

Perhaps this is not a very realistic fantasy. After all, I have never come across anyone with the surname "Up", let alone a doctor. I did however once know a Doctor Cute. I like the sound of "Cute's syndrome" too.

"Please excuse my son. He has Cute's."

Still, it could have been worse I suppose; there have been many other doctors with even worse names. If Marvel superhero and sorcerer Dr Strange had made the breakthrough then there would be paediatricians around the world who had to tell the new parents that their child has "Strange syndrome". Then there was Dr Octopus; I think most people would assume that a child with "Octopus syndrome" had eight legs.

"Doom syndrome" would be pretty bad too. Luckily Dr Doom was always far too busy planning global domination and the downfall of Reed Richards and the Fantastic Four to get involved in the field of learning disabilities. Just as well really - he probably would have enslaved them all and forced them to do his evil bidding.

These are fictional doctors of course, but what about Dr Spock? That's Benjamin Spock, the paediatrician, not Mr Spock the Star Trek character. Being an actual real person clearly makes Dr Spock the most likely candidate I have mentioned so far to have been involved in something like Down's syndrome. If it had been named after him though, most people would assume that people with "Spock's syndrome" had pointy ears and an inability to transcend logic.

Meg tells me she once knew a "Doctor Smelly"!

But anyway, we are stuck with "Down's syndrome".

By all accounts he was a nice man, Dr Down; he supported women's rights and racial equality, which was unusual for a Victorian gentleman.   However, we do also have Dr Down to blame for the word "Mongoloid". When he first discovered the condition, for some reason, because of the facial characteristics associated with it, he thought it was something to do with the race of people from Mongolia. He classified the condition as the "Mongolian type of Idiocy". Once again, I suppose it could have been worse. He could have thought they looked French.

Autistic Spectrum Disorder is a bit trickier to define. It is a disability caused by brain irregularities, that affects social and communication skills.

The word "autistic" comes from the Greek word "autos", which means "self", and reflects how autistic people are very self-absorbed.

The phrase "spectrum disorder" simply means that the way the symptoms affect people vary greatly from person to person, from mild to severe. It has nothing whatsoever to do with broken 1980s home computers.

Many autistic people have obsessive behaviour, very narrow interests, and sometime suffer from acute anxiety. Some people have intellectual difficulties, others are highly advanced in some areas (e.g. gifted in mathematics, music, or art), but struggle to interact with the world.

Many parents of autistic children say they find it difficult to deal with them in public because the fact that the child is on the autistic spectrum is not visibly apparent, and to a stranger, an autistic child who has become anxious just looks as though he/she is being naughty.

Jamie was diagnosed as being on the autistic spectrum when he was four years old. By then of course, we had come to terms with the Down's syndrome, and the fact that he was going to need care for the rest of his life, so another condition added to the mix did not seem to make much difference. My main thought when I was told was simple "that explains a lot". In truth, the autism affects Jamie's life just as much as the Down's Syndrome, maybe more. However, perhaps because we knew about the Down's Syndrome first, or perhaps because it is easier to understand, or maybe just because it can be seen on his face, I always focus on that as his main condition, both in this book and in everyday life.

Jamie's autism manifests itself in several ways. He has very little speech, preferring to communicate using single words or short phrases. He rarely uses gestures or facial expressions when communicating. He prefers to play alone, and has little interest in other children - he doesn't like them coming into his personal space. He has a set routine and he does get upset if that routine is broken. He also has some troubling behaviours, such as an insistence on spreading all his toys over as wide a surface area as possible, or lining them up; and the way he will repeat activities again and again.

One behaviour that has had a big impact on my own life, is his obsession with watching TV shows and movies over and over again. The movie *Toy Story 3* was the particular focus of his obsession for a few years. Before Jamie was born, I would sometimes watch a movie more than once if I really liked it, occasionally more than twice. *The Blues Brothers* held the record – it was my favourite film when I was a teenager and I watched it 15 times. That seemed like a lot at the time. By my calculations, I estimate I have now watched *Toy Story 3* on DVD with Jamie around 300 times. That is probably more than the director of

Toy Story 3 (Lee Unkrich, I did not need to look that up) has seen it.

It's a great movie, I recommend it. I loved it, the first few times. When it first came out, I remember how happy we were, because we were so sick of watching *Toy Story* and *Toy Story 2* on DVD (around 100 times each) and we thought it would make a nice change. If only we had known.

I used to try to wean Jamie off the *Toy Story* movies, just for my own sanity. I tried to get him into *The Jungle Book*, because I liked the songs, but it did not seem to appeal to him. I even tried to get him to watch *Groundhog Day* over and over again, just for the irony value, but he did not go for that either.

I seem to have wandered off the subject a little there. What I want to get across to you is that Jamie is a very unusual child. If you are a parent of a child who has recently been diagnosed with either Down's syndrome or Autistic Spectrum Disorder, I don't want you to panic. Your child will not be like Jamie. What we experienced with Jamie won't happen with you. Rather, you should read about our misadventures, laugh, and say to yourself:

"My future cannot possibly be as bad as what happened to those poor sods. Anyway, they seem to see the funny side about it now, so it cannot have been too bad."

I would love to be able to offer you advice, but despite having more than a decade's experience, I still don't feel qualified. Every child and every family is different. I can only tell you about what happened to us, and hope that it helps a little.

If you are not a parent of a child who has recently been diagnosed with either Down's syndrome or Autistic Spectrum Disorder, and you are just reading this because you liked the cover, you can just read about our misadventures, laugh, and leave it at that.

Yes, it is okay to laugh at this book; it is supposed to be funny. Over the next dozen or so chapters I might occasionally share a poignant moment or two – chapter 4 in particular is rather downbeat, but don't be disheartened, it will soon be over; and also the story in the penultimate chapter ("The Accident") is one I am not ready to laugh about yet, but that is ages away. Generally though I hope this book will be considered an entertaining read. It is not a misery memoir. I know that a lot of people who have family members with Down's syndrome, especially going back a generation or two, have had a terrible time dealing with the authorities and society as a whole, but that has simply not been our experience. All the professionals we have come into contact with over the years have been decent people; I cannot bring myself to rail against even the slightly hopeless ones. However, as I write this, I am considering implying in the Amazon blurb that our lives have been one long struggle against cold and heartless authority figures, as I believe that might help to improve my sales.

I could not write a mis mem, because I know that Jamie has been an exceptionally lucky boy. He was lucky to be born in a country and an era in which society as a whole wants to help disabled people and their families as much as it can. And he was lucky to be born into a family that loves him.

Both sets of grandparents, despite neither of them living on the doorstep, do all they can for him, and us. Sometimes it is babysitting, sometimes providing emotional support, sometimes fixing things around the house that Jamie has broken (something that, for some reason, I seem to be incapable of doing myself).

Where Jamie really got lucky though, was in having Meg for a mother. Nobody could have cared more and done more than she has. This book is written from my perspective, so there is a danger that someone could read it and think that I was the one who was involved in all the main events of Jamie's life, and deserve all the credit for raising him. I want to make it clear now that that is not the case. If ever I go a few pages without mentioning Meg, please just assume that she was there somewhere, in the background, holding everything together.

Our lives have not worked out the way we thought they would, they are crazy and chaotic, but we love our son more than life itself, and we want to celebrate him and tell his story.

Chapter 3: S & M

(That's Steve and Meg. Sorry if that disappoints you, but it is not that sort of book either.)

Before we go any further, I feel that this is the point in the book where I should backtrack a little and tell you about myself. I have read a few memoirs over the years, and it seems to be the done thing.

My name is Steve. Or you can call me Stephen if you prefer – I answer to both. I am not going to tell you how old I am, but let us just say I am close to a significant milestone that a lot of people dread. And when I say "close to" I mean that in the sense that I recently passed it. And when I say "recently" I mean ... no, never mind that. I have said too much already.

I sense this is going to be a difficult chapter for me. The problem is that I don't really like writing about myself. Like most writers I would dearly love to come across as cool, clever, and sophisticated, but it is so difficult to get that right. If I write at great length about all my many impressive achievements, you would think I was arrogant and big-headed, but if I take a modest approach I will feel as though I have done myself a disservice. It could be worse I suppose – I could actually have many impressive achievements that I desperately want you to know about without my having to mention them, but luckily I just have a few unimpressive ones.

An obvious solution to my dilemma would be to ask Meg to write about me. It would be an interesting literary device to have more than one narrator in a memoir, I think, but the problem is that I don't trust Meg to make me seem cool. She would probably tell you about the time I fainted during a particularly graphic discussion about the symptoms of various venereal diseases. You would never think I was cool if you heard that story. The other thing she might do is tell you about the time I laughed at her when she tried to walk up the down escalator in Boots (that's the shop, not the footwear) in Cheltenham town centre, thereby making me seem cruel and heartless. I am in fact neither cruel nor heartless, it really was very funny – you had to be there.

What I wanted to get across to you, hopefully without sounding like a dick, is how much I was brought up to value academic excellence. I did well at school from an early age and found I really enjoyed the praise I got from parents and teachers. I was top of my class in primary school, and I was regional chess champion (oh dear, there go a few more cool points).

I passed the entrance exam to the top school in the North of England, where I joined a hundred or so other high achievers, and I was top of my class there too (well, one time I was). I went to Oxford University to read mathematics (well, I went for an *interview* to read mathematics at Oxford University, but I blew it by panicking over a relatively simple question about the 1001 times table). While studying for my maths degree I used to read Shakespeare and Dickens in my spare time. After university I got a job in the south west of England, doing sums for a big multi-national financial institution. I have been doing that, or something similar, for over twenty years now, so there is a good chance I won't be able to stop myself from putting a pie chart into this book at some point later on – force of habit, you see.

I have just reread that previous paragraph to myself and I suspect you probably have an image of me in your head now, and I don't think it is a fair one; so I just want to add that I have no interest in Dungeons and Dragons (any more), I do *not* wear a bow tie and glasses (well, hardly ever), and I have never been to a Star Trek convention (though in all honesty, if they ever held one in Gloucestershire I would be sorely tempted).

Hmmm. Perhaps I should have let Meg write this after all.

The point I am trying to make is that I think the fact that I came from such an academic background made it more difficult for me to come to terms with Jamie's Down's syndrome. In the months before he was born I had given a lot of thought as to what sort of father I was going to be, and how I was going to try to help him follow in my footsteps. I had a dream that I would coach him in mathematics, or whatever subject he felt passionately about, and maybe he would surpass me and actually get into Oxford University. I was going to be supportive and nurturing rather than demanding and forceful. I would be the teacher who would help him reach his full potential, like *Dead Poets Society* but with less standing on the furniture. Maybe he would be a doctor, a world famous historian, a professor of economics, or a great novelist. That was all taken away from Jamie, and from me, in an instant.

Meg is clever too, but in a different way. She was not as academically motivated as me. She once told me that she went into her English Literature A-level without actually having read the set text. It was *A Passage to India*, and she claims she could not get past the chapter with the "bridge party". She knew that the bridge party was not a success, but nothing beyond that. If most of the questions in the exam had been about the first hundred pages, she might have gotten away with it. Unfortunately for her, the person setting the exam had actually finished reading the book, and the questions he/she set reflected that fact. Fortunately for her though, she had already been accepted into nursing college and did not need to do well in her A levels.

Yes, Meg is a nurse. She was a student nurse when I met her. She was well known in Cheltenham General Hospital for two things. The first was for producing some of the finest essays ever seen there – years later they were still being used as model answers. The second thing was the time she misheard a request for a "teeth pot" (a small receptacle for storing the patient's dentures in) and turned up in the middle of a cardiac arrest with a *teapot*, on a tray. Also on the tray were the hospital's best china teacups, and biscuits. They were Jammy Dodgers.

Despite this second thing (which sadly, I am sure, was talked about far more than the first thing) she did qualify as a nurse, and, according to many of her patients that I spoke to over the years, was a fantastic one. Whenever she was on duty, her patients knew they were going to be okay.

It was actually at Cheltenham General Hospital that I met Meg for the first time. She was the (student) nurse on duty when I took my friend Max in to the A&E department after he dropped a paving stone onto his hand. I will always remember the first time I saw Meg – her beautiful figure, pretty face, and warm smile. The nurse's uniform had nothing to do with it.

If you have not been to a hospital for a while and your only experience of the uniform is hen parties and *Carry On Doctor*, then your expectations will be all wrong - the truth is that modern nurses' uniforms are basically aprons, and the overall look is not entirely dissimilar to the uniform of a school dinner lady. So, no, it was not the uniform that drew me to her – it was her perfect skin, her ready wit, and her sunny disposition. I have always felt a little bad for Max – I got to meet the love of my life that day, and all he got was three broken fingers, which would have seriously affected his love life for the worse.

By the way, I want to promise you at this point that all of the stories I have told you, or am about to tell you, are completely true, or at the very least almost completely true. I have hardly exaggerated at all. A few of the names in the stories have been changed, and one person is an amalgam, but that's all.

Speaking of changed names though, I should mention that Meg's real name is not actually Meg. Her real name is Lisa. This is not one of the names I changed for the book (if it had been then the fact I have just told you her real name would have been a bit strange) it is just that I have always called her Meg. The story is that when she was a student and she first moved into the nurses' residence, the student who had occupied the room before her was called Meg, and Meg (by whom I mean Lisa, sorry if this is confusing) never got round to removing her name from the bedroom door. After a while, the other nurses decided that the name Meg suited her better than Lisa, and everybody started calling her that. And I mean everybody. When I first met her in Cheltenham A&E, her name badge said "Meg", not "Lisa". We had been dating for several months before I actually found out her real name. It was when I met her parents, and as I recall it took me longer than it should have done to figure out who this Lisa person was that they kept talking about. I still call her Meg to this day though – the nurses were right, it does suit her better.

Three years after we started dating, we were married in a fairy-tale castle in the middle of a forest. Then we became the sort of couple who you would probably hate - we were young, confident, and happy. We ate in fine restaurants, had cool friends, wore nice clothes, and travelled the world.

I mention this because I think it is an important context for our story. Before Jamie was born we thought our lives were going to be perfect. Everything leading up to that point had made us think that we led charmed lives; nothing could touch us. We were mistaken.

Things began to go wrong when we started trying to have a baby. Meg suffered miscarriage after miscarriage, and we were beginning to think that it was never going to happen for us. We began to talk about adoption. Eventually though, one of the pregnancies lasted longer than any of the others before it, and we realised that this time, it was going to be different. Champagne was bought, parents were told, and the spare room was turned into a nursery. We were back on track.

One Sunday afternoon, I took the heavily pregnant Meg out to the local multiplex cinema. We were in a celebratory mood as the pregnancy was going well, and there were no signs of any problems. We settled into our seats and started watching the trailers. Meg took a drink from the big paper cup of lemonade that she had bought at the concession stand, and when she had had enough, she balanced it on her stomach, using the pregnancy bump as an impromptu table. She nudged me, and when I looked over, she grinned. "Do you wish you had a table?" she said, and held her hands up as if to say "look no hands" while the drink balanced on her stomach. This was the moment that Jamie chose to make his presence known. From inside the womb he delivered a kick that knocked the cup over, and spilled its contents over Meg's legs. Meg, delighted and horrified in equal parts, shrieked and leapt to her feet. Other people in the cinema turned to see what was going on, and I imagine that when they saw a heavily pregnant lady standing there, looking surprised and excited, and dripping wet below the waist with a clear fluid, they expected that they were about to witness something even more dramatic than the movie they had paid to see. Perhaps they were going to see a live birth, or at the very least, a pair of panicking parents rushing out of the cinema towards the maternity wing of the nearby hospital. I assume they were a bit confused then, when all we did was dry Meg off with paper towels, then settle back down into our seats again.

Throughout the rest of the pregnancy, we retold that story to anyone who would listen. We found it hilarious that the unborn child had managed to spill a drink, and joked that when he was born he was going to have some sort of special drink-spilling superpower. I wonder now if Jamie heard all this, and thought to himself "Laugh it up suckers. I'll be seeing you soon."

Jamie had started as he intended to go on.

Chapter 4: The Worst Week

"Did you know he had Down's syndrome before he was born?"

That's the question that most people ask us, sooner or later. Perhaps they are curious as to whether or not we considered having a termination - that is, they want to know whether or not we had "chosen" the lifestyle. Or perhaps they just want to picture in their heads the moment we found out, and want to get the details of the mental image just right. Either way, they should mind their own business and not ask such personal questions.

Since it does seem to be a subject that interests people though, I have decided to tell you about it. I have already mentioned that I want this book to be a bit of fun - a celebration of our chaotic lives - but unfortunately this part of the story is not going to be fun. Let's get it out of the way quickly shall we? The day they told me my son had Down's syndrome was the worst day of my life, and even now, years later, the memory is not pleasant.

To answer the question, no, we did not know about Jamie's condition before he was born. We had been offered a prenatal test, but were warned that the test did carry a small risk of damage to the baby. We had discussed it and decided that whatever condition the baby had, we would want to keep it anyway, so why risk it? We opted out.

Instead then, it was the day after Jamie was born that we found out. Meg and I were sat on the bed, feeling happier than ever before, holding our little boy between us. We had been given a private room in the maternity ward after the birth; at the time we naively thought that it was a professional courtesy, with Meg being a nurse. The doctor came in; he was all smiles as he took the baby from us and carried out his little tests. -He listened to the heartbeat, checked reflexes and inspected hands and feet. He was still all smiles as he told us that the boy's heart and reflexes were fine and that we had a beautiful healthy baby. He wondered if we had any questions. There was something about his use of language that made me uneasy. He seemed to be focussing on health a lot, but had not said the word "perfect", or even "normal", and he seemed to be avoiding mentioning the baby's mental condition.

"Well," I said, "you've told us he's physically healthy, but how does he seem mentally to you? I mean, there's no sign of anything like brain damage, or Down's syndrome... is there?"

I knew it was a strange thing to ask, but I just wanted to be reassured that everything was as it should be, so that my happiness could be complete. I did not really think that there was anything wrong with Jamie. True, I had thought that his eyes had seemed a little bit narrow, but since all the doctors and midwives had seemed so happy for us up until that point, I had dismissed the thought. As the doctor started to answer my question though, I noticed that his hands were shaking. He was still smiling, but the words he was saying were all wrong. I remember hearing "...many of the characteristics associated with Down's syndrome..." and then I heard Meg wail. I suddenly felt weak and flopped onto the bed, vaguely aware that the doctor was showing us something on the baby's hands and feet. He had stopped smiling.

So that is how it happened. I warned you it was not a barrel of laughs. The following days and weeks were also pretty harrowing.

It may not have been an actual bereavement, but it felt like one. In my mind I had had a son - he was good looking, funny, wise and successful. I was looking forward to watching him grow up, and I could already feel my pride as I attended those parent-teacher meetings. He would become a confident young man, leading an interesting life; I was looking forward to hearing stories of his round-the-world travelling, swimming with sharks on the Great Barrier Reef.

Even though he had never actually existed, to me that person had died. And I had to grieve.

The five stages of grief, according to somebody I will look up on Wikipedia one day, are denial, bargaining, anger, depression, and acceptance. Until now I had always been very sceptical about this. I had always thought that surely not everybody responds to tragedy in the same way. It was with morbid curiosity then, and actually a little amusement, that I watched myself go through each of the stages in turn.

Denial lasted for a few days. I argued that a lot of people on my side of the family had narrow eyes, and a lot of people on Meg's side had big hands. I have a big gap between my two biggest toes too. I kept coming back to the fact that the doctor had originally told us that he might be wrong in his diagnosis. I was sure he was wrong. There was nothing wrong with my boy! It wasn't until the third day when the hospital's top consultant put his arm round me and said "I'm sorry, but I really don't think there's any doubt" that I began to accept it. Even after that I occasionally found myself fantasizing about how embarrassed the doctors would be, and how happy we would be, when the test results came back negative. I had even decided that I wouldn't sue anybody!

A day or two later I heard myself saying to a relative that this experience had been such a revelation to me, that even if the test results did come back negative, I would like to do some volunteer work with Down's children. Then I burst out laughing as I realised I was in the bargaining stage.

The anger phase was quite short lived. I couldn't get angry with the doctors and nurses because they were all so good. I couldn't be angry with Meg or my family because I cared about them all too much and they were suffering as much as I was. Instead, I found myself getting angry with the outside world - a millionaire football manager practically in tears because he'd been sacked, lorry drivers protesting about the cost of fuel, American idiots yelling at each other on talk shows - what right did any of these people have to be miserable? I wished that my biggest problem was that I'd lost my job, or that petrol was a bit dear, or that my mother dressed like a whore. After that I started to feel angry towards women who had had healthy babies. I just knew that some of them had smoked and drank during pregnancy, and that many of them would be lousy parents; they did not deserve a normal healthy baby, and it just wasn't fair.

But that soon passed. I'm not sure whether the depression stage started before or after the test results came back. By the time we got the results we already knew what they were going to be. It wasn't a shock -

by then I just felt numb. I had no energy and no interest in anything, I just wanted to sleep all the time.

I saw the rest of my life stretched out before me with dread; filled with drudgery, bitterness and disappointment.

One night, a few days after Jamie had been born, I was on my way to the hospital to visit him in intensive care, I stopped at some traffic lights on the outskirts of the town, and looked up to my left to see a giant advertising billboard. The advert on the poster was for a particular brand of baby milk that claimed to make your child more intelligent. It featured a young baby, a few months old, wearing a nappy. The baby had been playing with alphabet blocks, and had arranged them to form a word. The word was "PAEDIATRICIAN".

As I looked at the poster I felt a small stab of anguish; I knew that Jamie was never going to be a clever child like that, and he was never going to grow up to be a paediatrician. He was never even going to be able to spell the word.

As the poignancy of the situation dawned on me, a song started playing on the car radio - a sad 80s power ballad - and I became aware of how I would appear to an observer at that point. I imagined myself as a character in a movie - a tear jerking drama in which I was played by some brooding hunk -

Robert Pattinson perhaps. His life had fallen apart, and the universe seemed to be mocking him; all the while the movie soundtrack reverberated around the cinema. It was even raining.

The traffic light changed to green. I decided to wait a little longer. I carried on sitting there, listening to the music, gazing forlornly at the giant super-baby that filled my field of vision, and properly feeling sorry for myself until the traffic light changed back to red again.

After a few minutes, I decided that I had sat and felt sorry for myself for long enough, and it was time to carry on with my journey. The song had ended, and an annoying local DJ was spoiling the mood by prattling on about petrol prices. The only problem was that the traffic light was still red. A few more minutes passed, and the light was still red; I was starting to feel a little awkward. I had always assumed that the traffic lights were in some sort of timed rotation, and they went from red to amber to green, and back, all day and all night. However, as the light in front of me refused to turn green, it occurred to me that perhaps the change was initiated by some sort of sensor that detected a car approaching. If this was the case, it was never going to turn green for me, because it had already detected my approach and, quite reasonably, assumed that I would have gone by now. I was going to have to sit there until another car arrived behind me and got picked up by the sensor. The only problem was, it was the middle of the night on a quiet road, and it could be half an hour before another car arrived. Even then, would the sensor detect it or would my own car block it?

Eventually, I put the car into gear, and jumped the red light. As I continued on my journey, I realized a few things for the first time. The first was that I had been a ridiculous boob ten minutes earlier. I had to snap out of this foolish wallowing in self-pity. There would be no more feeling sorry for myself – the depression phase was over – I was now at acceptance. The second realization was that life is not like the movies; perhaps this is just as well otherwise there would have been a cop car that saw me jump the red light, and there would have been a car chase possibly culminating in a shoot-out ending in tragedy and Jamie would have had to grow up without a father. The final realization was that if they ever did make a movie of my life, it would be a comedy. I would not be played by Robert Pattinson, it would be Simon Pegg.

That week was the worst one of my life. Meg felt the same.

We both agree though, that if we had known then what we know now, things would not have seemed anything like as bleak.

Chapter 5: Upside Downs

In the spirit of "looking on the bright side", here are the top ten good things about having a child like Jamie:

(I am pretty sure that there are no other children like Jamie, but just go with me for now)

1. He will be happy.

The first thing I thought about when I found out about Jamie's Down's syndrome was how it would affect me, and how it would affect Meg. If I had known how it would actually affect Jamie, I would not have been so upset. Jamie had a great childhood – better than anybody's I have ever known. He had so much fun, he laughed all the time, he was happy. He was happier than Larry, the famous millionaire pig with two tails who lived in a palace made from his own excrement.

When Jamie was a baby, I worried about how tough it must be being a kid these days. There is so much violence around, and I feared Jamie would be bullied when he was older. I would do my best to protect him; I had a put-down line up my sleeve in case I ever heard any kids laughing at him or being mean.

"He has got an extra chromosome. What's your excuse?"

That was the put-down line. I have never needed it. Jamie has never been bullied.

I was having a conversation with a more experienced dad about this subject one day, and he told me that I had nothing to worry about, that kids like Jamie don't get bullied. He told me that even the nastiest teenager would draw the line at that. There is nothing cool about bullying a kid with Down's syndrome – it is not the way a bully would choose to impress his cronies.

By not being bullied, Jamie avoided one of the most traumatic parts of childhood. And that was not the only trauma he avoided – he never experienced jealously, he never worried about the future, he never felt pressure to study for exams, and he never felt unwanted.

2. He will be cool.

Well, I suppose that depends on your definition of cool. If you are old enough to remember the 1970s then it will be difficult for you to hear the word "cool" without visualising Arthur Fonzerelli in a black leather jacket and greased black hair, telling grown-up squares to sit on it. Times have changed though; *Happy Days* was a long time ago.

When I was a teenager, I did think it was my duty to at least make the effort to be a little bit cool. I found it difficult sometimes to reconcile this with my love of comic books, computer games, 19th century literature, and advanced mathematics, but I did my best, dammit. Sometimes I got it right, other times I got it wrong. For example, I was a regular at rock concerts and festivals, but I spoiled it by calling my mum to tell her I was okay.

Looking back, I now realise that the very fact I was trying to be cool meant that I was doomed to failure from the beginning. To be truly cool, it is not enough to make it look effortless, it actually has to <u>be</u> effortless.

Jamie has never made any effort whatsoever to be cool. I do have a photo of him in a black leather jacket with the collar up and shades on, but I dressed him like that, he had nothing to do with it, so it doesn't count. No, Jamie doesn't care what anyone else thinks of him, and he especially doesn't care what anyone thinks he looks like. Despite his nonchalance, he does always look good, partly due to his natural good looks and partly due to the fact that his mother spends more on fine clothes for him than she spends on herself. He looks good, but he does not care.

Effortless. Also, he does his own thing, regardless of what other people expect of him. He lives his life his way. How cool is that?

3. Nice People

Over the years, Jamie has brought us into contact with some of the nicest people imaginable – people who we would never otherwise have met.

A lot of these people are Jamie's respite carers, health professionals, social workers, and people who work at the special needs school that Jamie attends. There often seems to be something special about people who work with disabled children; I suspect this is because it is the sort of career that decent people gravitate towards, and only the most saint-like actually get the jobs. It could possibly be the other way around though – that is, working with disabled children actually turns you into a better person.

This brings me to my next point, which is that being Jamie's dad has made me a better person. It has become a Hollywood cliché where a cocky career-driven yuppie suddenly finds him/herself in a caring role and gains perspective on life and learns the true meaning of Christmas, or something; but it is a cliché for a reason – it really does happen.

4. Immunity

It seems to me that no matter how badly Jamie behaves, no other adult will ever tell him (or indeed us, his parents) off. I imagine that I would have received a stern rebuke if, when I was thirteen, I had forced my way into a neighbour's house, ran up their stairs, pulled down my pants and sat on their toilet. I might possibly have received a cuff around the ear. When Jamie did the same thing last year though, it was met with an amused chuckle; the neighbours had a good laugh with me when I came running up to their back door a few seconds behind Jamie, out of breath, and with an apologetic expression on my face.

I have been in situations where Jamie's victim has taken a few seconds to realize that he has Down's syndrome, and in those few seconds I have had a glimpse of what it must be like to be the parent of an ordinary delinquent child. Once, at a car-boot sale, a middle-aged woman started telling Jamie off because of some misdemeanour he had committed, when the younger woman she was with whispered something in her ear, and the telling-off stopped immediately. The older woman then apologized to me and shuffled off.

Another time, in a soft-play area, a parent came up to me to complain, not unreasonably, that Jamie had been spitting at her child at the top of the spiral slide; she only got as far as explaining the facts when two of her friends dragged her away telling her to leave me alone. After she had gone, a bystander congratulated me on what a great job I was doing.

You see? It is immunity. It is just as well really, or else we would all be in prison by now.

5. Free Parking Anywhere You Want

...well, anywhere except a taxi rank.

I found out about the taxi rank exception the hard way. It was about a week after getting the "blue badge". I had just popped in to the butchers on the high street for two minutes and left my family in the car, and when I returned there was an ominous sticker on the windscreen. Apparently Meg had wondered why the traffic warden was taking so much interest in the car, stood in front of it and writing in his pad for a good thirty seconds, but she had not considered actually switching to the driver's seat and driving away before he had time to issue the fine. After paying that fine I think it took me about six months of not having to pay for car parks before I was back in credit again.

Anyway, apart from that, being able to use the disabled spaces is brilliant. Being allowed to park on double-yellow lines is quite surreal; it seems a bit too good to be true. I have never understood it. Surely if there are double yellow lines on the road that means it is not a good idea to park there, doesn't it? So why make exceptions? Every time I do park on double-yellows, whenever I return to the car I expect to find a little sticker on it telling me I have misunderstood the rules, and all the money I have saved in parking charges over the past six months has gone again.

On a similar theme, being able to use the disabled toilets whenever your child needs to pee when you are out and about is also a great thing. I know that if you are a parent of a recently diagnosed disabled child you will be thinking to yourself now that the permission to use slightly bigger toilet cubicles seems like a poor recompense for the terrible thing that has happened to your loved one; trust me though, when everything has settled down and you have come to terms with the situation, you will one day find yourself in the nicest public toilet you have ever seen in your life, and you will say to yourself that maybe things aren't so terrible after all.

6. An Excuse

If you are under 30, you might find it difficult to understand this, but once you reach a certain age, the idea of regularly going out pubbing and clubbing doesn't seem so appealing any more. If you try to tell a friend that you don't fancy going out one evening, he/she might try to badger you into changing your mind, but if you quietly imply that your disabled child is going through a difficult time at the moment they will quickly back off. If you are female, or just really in touch with your feminine side, you could try forcing out a tear for good measure.

(If you are one of my old friends reading this, and I once blew you off because of something to do with Jamie, I can assure you it was a genuine emergency that time.)

7. Theme Parks

Big amusement parks have special rules for disabled visitors. If you can produce a letter from a doctor and a disabled badge, they will give you a special pass that allows you to jump the queues, and enter the rides via a special disabled entrance. This special pass is one of the best things in the world ever. If you are considering going to a big amusement park, I recommend taking a disabled person with you.

The only downside is that you are only allowed to queue-jump if the disabled person is actually going on the ride with you. This means that when we went to Alton Towers a few years ago, I did not get to go on *Nemesis* at all, but I did have to go on *Frog Hopper* three times.

"Again daddy! Again!"

8. No Sports

Jamie's special needs school doesn't seem to go in for competitive sports. In a meeting once at the school, Meg suggested that they have a sports day there, and everyone looked at her as though she had suggested ethnic cleansing. Anyway, at least this means we don't have to go and pretend to enjoy watching him play football once a week in the rain, like my parents did with me. Poor sods. We never even used to win.

Obviously, if you are Usain Bolt and you are reading this, the idea that your child won't be following in your footsteps and doing sport might not seem like such a good thing. Let us be realistic though, you are not Usain Bolt.

9. Extended Childhood

It is easy to focus on the downside of having a child that develops slowly, but there is also an upside. How many times have you heard a parent complain that "They grow up so quickly these days"? Our next-door neighbour was telling me not so long ago how upset she was that her nine year old daughter no longer believed in Santa Claus, and so now the magic was over for both of them. Not so with Jamie – I don't think he will ever figure out that (spoiler alert – if you don't want to know the truth about the dark conspiracy at the heart of Christmas and want to continue living a lie, look away now) it is actually his dad behind that fake white beard.

And what about the movies? Once normal kids reach a certain age they think they are too cool for family movies. Not Jamie though. Thanks to him Meg and I had an excuse to see some great movies at the cinema. Pixar and Disney movies today are really great. I genuinely believe that *Monsters' University* was the funniest film of 2013, but because it is supposed to be a kids' film, I would not have gone to see it without Jamie. I might have gone to see *The Hangover Part 3* instead, and that just doesn't bear thinking about.

The fears that haunt most parents of teenagers don't bother me at all. I cannot ever imagine Jamie getting into drugs, impregnating his girlfriend, or crashing his motorbike.

10. Cuddles

This is the best one. How many dads still get long enthusiastic cuddles from their teenage children? I do. Admittedly, Jamie can get a little carried away sometimes. On these occasions they stop being "cuddles" and become "CUDDLES!" If you want to visualize what a CUDDLE! is like, go to You-Tube and look up "Rod Hull and Emu on Parkinson", and you will get an idea.

When it is just a cuddle though, it is delightful. Jamie and I have had a lot of practice cuddling each other, and we have become really good at it. He will happily lie on the sofa with me for half an hour watching TV while I read a book. Sometimes he will fall asleep in my arms, other times he will wait until I am not expecting it, then knock the book out of my hands. You just never know.

****

So there you are. Ten good things.

I actually feel better about my life now having written this chapter. I don't think I will bother with a chapter called "Ten bad things". I am sure I could do it but this is not a misery memoir.

Chapter 6: Things People Say

As soon as Jamie was out of hospital, I realized I was going to have to tell all my friends and work colleagues the news about his condition. I actively tried to avoid doing this, and my mum and dad, who were staying with us, helped out. They told my boss at work, plus a few well-wishers who turned up unexpectedly on the doorstep. I had to tell Max myself though, because he, for some reason, thought that it would be acceptable to find out whether or not everything had gone okay by phoning me from his car using his fancy new (at the time) "hands free" set. This meant that I had to shout the news to him down the phone. I had to shout it twice in fact, as he did not hear it the first time over the noise of the engine and the traffic. When he finally understood what I was saying, he was at a loss for words. Eventually he just said "Oh dear" to which I replied "Yes" and hung up.

Despite my reluctance to talk about it, I still found myself having "the conversation" on a regular basis over the next few weeks.

If I could have my time again, I think I would have bingo cards printed up, so that Meg and I could play

Down's syndrome cliché bingo. The squares on the cards would include the following things that were said to me, or Meg, time after time:

- They are very loving
- Some of them are very musical
- Did you know beforehand…?
- Wherever did he get his ginger hair from?
- Special children go to special parents
- It's all part of God's plan
- Everything happens for a reason
- It's just a label
- He's still your son
- You would not have him any other way
- It's like going to Holland

That last item on the list refers to a famous article written by Emily Perl Kingsley, the mother of a boy with Down's syndrome, in 1987. In the article Emily draws an analogy, saying that having a child with Down's syndrome is a bit like planning a big holiday to Italy, only to have the plane unexpectedly redirected to Holland. Emily's point is that although it might not be the glamorous destination you were hoping for, and now you have to learn Dutch instead of Italian, one must not fall into despair, because it is still quite possible to have a great time in Holland. She mentions windmills.

When I first heard this story, I remember being a bit unkind about it. I pointed out that I had once actually been to Holland, while InterRailling round Europe with Max in the 1990s, and had not liked it at all. We were almost mugged in Amsterdam and there were dildos in the shop windows. And I never saw any windmills. I might also have mentioned how weird it is that there are no connecting flights, or indeed trains, between Holland and Italy. Is there some sort of international emergency going on? A hurricane? A viral outbreak? A zombie apocalypse?

I feel a bit bad about reacting the way I did, deliberately missing the point. Looking back now, years later, I can see that the analogy is actually a very good one. I know that it has helped hundreds of people over the years. If Emily had said Switzerland though, instead of Holland, I would have been with her from the start. Switzerland is the home of Toblerone, cheese with holes in it, and the greatest mathematician of all time, Leonhard Euler (well it was his home; he is dead now, but his pioneering work on exponential functions lives on).

A few people we met in the early days did manage to avoid the clichés, and come up with something we had not heard before. They had varying degrees of success.

Claire, a nurse friend of Meg's tried to add a little humour. This was always going to be a high risk strategy. She came round to visit us at our home in the first week. She already knew about Jamie's Down's syndrome, but had not actually seen him. When Meg opened the door to her, she came in, smiled, and said to Meg "Never mind, at least he's not ginger." This did not get the laugh she was hoping for, on account of the fact that, as you might recall, Jamie actually is ginger. Meg told me that she felt so bad for her friend's mistake, that she briefly considered just laughing and then quickly putting a hat on Jamie before introducing him to Claire. However, to really see this through she would have to make sure he was wearing a hat every time Claire saw him, and that seemed like a lot of effort to go to.

Another time, a woman in the park commented on Jamie while Meg was pushing him on the swings. She said "He's such a gift, isn't he?" This was when Jamie was a toddler, and at the height of his adorableness, so Meg just smiled and nodded; if the conversation had happened a few years later though, at the height of the difficult behaviour, she might have muttered something about wishing someone had kept the receipt.

One young mother we told about Jamie tried to sympathise with us by sharing their own family problems. "I know just how you feel," she said, "I have just found out that my son Nathan has to wear glasses."

The strangest thing that anyone ever said to us was "Maybe he will grow up to marry someone who fell out of a tree." It was an elderly neighbour who said this. After Meg and I interrogated her for a few minutes, we eventually figured out what it was that she was trying to say. She told us that she used to know a woman who had fallen out of a tree as a child, and had never been quite right since. That woman had eventually married a man who had Down's syndrome. I am not sure why the elderly neighbour thought this story would help us. Was she suggesting that somewhere out there, there might be a brain damaged young girl (specifically, brain damaged from falling out of a tree) who would be our future daughter in law? Something to look forward to eh?

It is easy for me to laugh at these people (fun too!) but the truth is I respect the fact that at least they tried. They did not just avoid us. Some old friends sent cards and presents in the post, and they were a help too. I am sure it was difficult deciding what to write in those cards. We got a lot of "Best Wishes", but not so many "Congratulations". That's fine though, they made the effort, and I appreciated it.

A few old friends did not get in touch though, and that disappointed me. At least, I think I was disappointed. The thing is, I hardly told anyone about Jamie's diagnosis at the time, I just assumed that word would spread through the grapevine (it seemed likely – one friend in particular who definitely did know was a terrible gossip), and that people who I had not spoken to in a few years would use it as an excuse to get it touch again. With a couple of exceptions though, it did not really happen. I did tell one old friend via a social network site, and she never replied to my message and I have never heard from her since. A couple of Meg's old friends were disappointments too. One said "I can't deal with this" and disappeared from our lives.

As the years went on, it became easier for me to talk about Jamie. Whenever I met a new person and they asked me about my family, I always tried to mention it early on. Not mentioning it can lead to awkward conversational cul-de-sacs. For example, I once had a conversation with someone whose name was probably something like Dave that went like this:

Dave:	"Have you got any children?"
Me:	"Yes, I have a little boy called Jamie."
Dave:	"What sort of things does he like to do?"
Me:	"Er…well…he likes watching CBeebies."

Dave:	"Oh right. When does he start school?"
Me:	"He's already started actually."
Dave:	"How old is he?"
Me:	"Nine."

After that day, whenever anybody asked me if I had children, I always answered:

"Yes, I have a little boy, called Jamie. He has Down's syndrome."

That often made the other person flinch a little, but I found that if I said it confidently and matter-of-factly, people took their lead from me, and didn't get embarrassed or try to offer sympathy.

It seems strange to me now that I remember so many details about conversations and remarks that were made more than a decade ago, but I do. It was an intense time.

Of all the things that were said to us about Jamie in the early years, there is one that stands out in my memory above all the others. It was just a passing comment, but it was not a cliché, it was a sincere and personal comment, and helped me feel better at the time more than any of the other comments. The person who said it was a colleague at work – an older lady, who I only knew slightly. She had heard about Jamie's diagnosis, and one day, as she was passing my desk, she stopped and spoke to me.

"I have six grandchildren." she said. "One of them has Down's syndrome…"

I looked up at her, and she leaned in conspiratorially, and whispered to me "…he's my favourite!"

I knew she was telling the truth.

Chapter 7: Year One

The first year of our life with Jamie was, I imagine, not dissimilar to a year in the life of many first-time parents. I know that there are a lot of parents who have babies who sleep through the night every night, need little attention, and are easily made happy. Those are not the parents I mean.

What I mean is that the first year of our life with Jamie was not dissimilar to the life of those first-time parents whose baby demands constant attention all day and all night, and would regard himself/herself as having failed if either parent ever slept for more than twenty minutes at a time.

I know that this is a common theme in parenting. I know that we were not alone. I think it is more common for a baby to be screaming for attention every time the miserable, exhausted parent nods off than it is for a baby to be a sound sleeper. I remember the reaction at work once when the father of a young baby casually mentioned that his child was a sound sleeper; the air turned blue for a few seconds as all the other parents told the young man exactly what they thought of him for mentioning this. It dawned on me then that babies seem to be genetically programmed to disturb their parents sleep patterns. I am not sure why this should be the case. What evolutionary advantage could there possibly be in having bleary-eyed young parents fighting fatigue while trying to keep their own lives going? Surely in prehistoric times, when predators roamed the Earth, having a screaming baby in the middle of the night announcing the family's exact location to all the hungry animals in the vicinity was not a great idea. You would have thought that in this context "survival of the fittest" would have meant "survival of the people who did not carry around with them a small thing that made a noise exactly like a dinner gong for lions and tigers and bears".

Eventually I noticed that Jamie often seemed to fall asleep on car journeys. Wrapped up in a blanket and lying down on his little car seat (which was the detachable crib section from his pram), he seemed to find the motion of the car and the vibrations from the engine soothing. Inevitably this discovery led to me taking him out for a drive every time we needed to get him to sleep. Sometimes it would only take a few minutes, other times it would take half an hour, but generally it seemed to work. We were very relieved to have finally found a technique that worked, though it was a bit of a chore having to go out driving late at night, every night.

I mentioned this to Max one Saturday afternoon when he dropped round, and he tried to persuade me that what I was doing was terrible for the environment. Max did not care about the environment, he was just trying to wind me up, and I seem to recall he compared my actions to the crimes of Saddam Hussein and Exxon Mobile. I laughed it off, of course, but in my heart I think I knew that at that point in my life the environment was not high on my priority list. I would willingly have sacrificed the entire ozone layer and all of the rainforests in the world just to get a decent night's sleep. The only pollution I cared about back then was noise pollution. On the other hand though, when Max gleefully started calculating how much money this extra petrol was costing me each week, I began to see that maybe he had a point, and perhaps it was my civic duty to look for alternative solutions.

The alternative solution we came up with was to give Jamie a dummy at bedtimes. He liked it, and it seemed to sooth him, so we could not see any harm in it. A few experts advised against it, but we thought we knew better. What did experts know? According to experts, the Titanic was unsinkable, Gary Barlow was going to have a better solo career than Robbie Williams, and you'll win nothing with kids.

Unfortunately, it seems they were right this time. Before long Jamie was demanding the dummy not just at bedtimes, but also during the day too. Jamie's speech was severely delayed as he grew up, and it seemed likely to me that the dummy was partly responsible. He was still using the dummy years later (many years later), even when we went out of the house. When you are in a restaurant, having a toddler sweetly ask his parents for a dummy is one thing, but having an angry ten year old shouting for a dummy like a junkie demanding a hit of crystal-meth is quite another. We should not have got Jamie hooked on dummies during that first year, but it was a difficult time, and we were desperate for anything that would make our lives easier.

Something that did make our lives easier during that first year, was the help my mum and dad gave us. I had been beginning to realise the full implications of my decision, ten years earlier, to leave my home town and move to the south. When I moved away I was thinking of my career, and of the excitement of a new start. What I was not thinking was that one day I would be in dire need of help from my parents, and they would not be around to give it. Jamie's condition had hit them hard too – he was their first grandchild, and they had had the same hopes and expectations for him that I had. Emotionally I am sure they were in a similar place to me and Meg. They really wanted to help us but they were four hour's drive away up the M1.

They were determined to help though. Within a few months they had taken early retirement and bought a little house just up the road from us. We were so lucky to have their support. They helped us so much with Jamie during the first year, and indeed the subsequent years, I don't know how we would have gotten through without them.

There is one other aspect that comes to mind in which we were lucky – very lucky - and that was Jamie's health. Half of all children with Down's syndrome are born with serious heart defects. These defects can have a profound effect on the child's quality of life, and life expectancy. Jamie was in the half who had healthy hearts. We found this out when he was just a few weeks old. I took him back to the hospital to be tested – it was the most important test we would ever be involved in – and it was good news. We had beaten the odds (does it count as beating the odds when it is 50/50? You would think I would know that being a statistician wouldn't you?).

A few weeks later I was listening to the radio when a story came on the news; scientists had discovered that something found in tuna fish was very good for the heart, and I remembered that Meg had had an insatiable craving for tuna when she was pregnant. I began to wonder if she had "fixed" Jamie's heart while he was in her womb. For just a few seconds I was filled with pride, and I wondered at the miracle of life, but then I heard the rest of the news story on the radio, and they pointed out that pregnant women should not eat too much tuna because of the high mercury levels in the fish. They did not say what the effect of the mercury would be on an unborn baby, and I decided not to look it up. It would only upset me if the symptoms turned out to be poor sleep patterns, addiction to dummies, and disruptive behaviour in public libraries.

If Meg had fixed Jamie's heart, it would only have been the first of many amazing things she did for him. Jamie could not have wished for a better mother. Despite being sleep deprived and full of all sorts of post-pregnancy hormones, Meg was determined to do everything she could to give him the best chance possible for a normal life. She took the view that if he was going to learn things at half the speed of a normal child, she would work twice as hard teaching him. As it turned out though, I think she worked ten times as hard. She gave up her nursing career and threw herself into the job of being Jamie's mother. Social services sent round a "portage worker" who taught her how best to play with him so that he learned while having fun, and so Meg became Jamie's play therapist.

They also sent a physiotherapist to us, who taught us how to teach Jamie how to walk. We had been told that most children with Down's syndrome take several years to learn how to walk, but Meg was not prepared to accept that, so she also became his full time physiotherapist.

I had to go back to work (and to be honest, I was glad to do so; I used to say that I was going to work for a rest, and I was only half joking), but I tried to do my bit at weekends. I would take over feeding and nappy-changing duties, and I would try to take Jamie out somewhere to "stimulate" him (this was important, apparently) and also to give Meg a break. At first I used to take him to zoos, museums and art galleries, and he would gaze in wonder at the animals, exhibits, and paintings, sometimes breaking into a little smile. After a while though, I realized that Jamie was stimulated by pretty much everything; if I took him to Sainsbury's, Tesco, or Waitrose, he would gaze in wonder at the bananas, the tins of macaroni cheese, and the fresh olives stuffed with sun-dried tomatoes, sometimes breaking into a little smile.

We used to think that we were both *determined* to help Jamie, but looking back, I wonder if *desperate* would have been a better word. We read everything we could get our hands on, looking for advice, and we would have done anything anyone suggested to us if we had thought there was the slightest chance it would help. We talked about it, and neither of us wanted to be in a position where in, say, ten years' time, we were looking back and wondering if Jamie would have benefitted from some exercise, treatment, or experience, that we had not given him. I am sure we wasted a lot of money on things that had no effect.

When Jamie was very young, his head was a little misshapen. It seemed to be a little flat at the back. We mentioned this to our doctor, and he told us that this was very common, and it was because Jamie was sleeping on his back, and his soft skull was moulding to fit the mattress. This sounded worrying to me – skulls should not be changing shape to fit the mattress; surely it should be the other way round? The doctor assured us it was very common though, and Jamie would soon grow out of it. Continuing with our "what do experts know?" approach, we took the advice of a friend instead, who told us that she had experienced something similar with her child, and that a cranial osteopath had helped. I had never heard of cranial osteopathy, and had no opinion as to whether it was proper science or charlatan quackery. It was expensive, but there was a chance it might help, so I made an appointment.

The osteopath was a very nice young lady. She seemed very professional, apart from the fact that she operated from a "clinic" in her parents' house. It was a nice house however, and she had certificates on the wall, so that made up for it, I guess.

Over the course of several weeks, Jamie had his skull gently manipulated by this young lady. Very gently, in fact. Sometimes she just appeared to be holding his head, and I wondered if she was doing anything at all.

A couple of months and a dozen or so sessions later, the osteopath told us that Jamie was a lot better now. Looking at him, I was not so sure; his head still seemed rather flat at the back. However, the osteopath had proof - she produced two photographs. Putting down the first one on the table in front of us, she said "This is a picture I took of Jamie just before the first session." We looked at the photo, and the misshaped head was clear to see. Then she put down the second photo, and said "I took this photo last week, and you can see a clear improvement." We both peered at the photo, looking for improvement, but not really seeing it. The head was still misshapen. There was an awkward silence. All three of us stared at the pictures. After a while, a furrow appeared on the osteopath's brow. Then she blushed a little. Eventually, she said "Hang on. I've got those the wrong way round..."

As I mentioned at the beginning of the chapter, I am sure that most of the things that we experienced in that first year of Jamie's life were the sort of things that many first time parents experience. The thing that made that first year different for us though, more intense and more emotional, is that those other parents knew that all their problems were just temporary ones. They knew that the baby was going to grow up soon, and they could look forward to having an adorable toddler running around the house, then a sweet child, then (and I guess they try not to think about this) a moody teenager who despises them, before finally, an adult who will be a friend for ever (especially if he/she needs to borrow money). We did not know any of that. We had no idea what to expect.

Although Jamie's condition was never far from our thoughts, we eventually settled into the routine of family life in a way that it was not the only thing we thought about. Jamie was a beautiful baby, and as a beautiful baby he could not help but warm our hearts every time he smiled at us. It was a pleasure just watching him crawling around the floor, playing with toys, even sleeping. I loved to feed him. I loved to play peek-a-boo. I loved blowing on his tummy (that was my favourite actually – if I had my way tummy blowing would replace the handshake as the standard form of initialising social interactions). I did not even mind changing his nappies; I found it quite satisfying in fact, cleaning all those nooks and crannies – a bit like polishing a car, just not as shiny.

And Meg just loves babies. Her face lights up whenever there is a baby in the vicinity. So her baby, a special baby who was going to need more care and more help than most other babies, was never going to be short of love.

By the way, in case you were wondering, Jamie did learn to walk before he was a year old. All those hours that Meg put in, despite doubters telling her she was wasting her time, paid off ("IN YOUR FACE, DOUBTERS!" she has asked me to say). It was a great achievement, both for Jamie and for Meg, and we were thrilled. Well, at first we were thrilled. Once the novelty had worn off, and the reality hit us that now Jamie was mobile and free to get up to mischief wherever he wanted to, we started to wonder if we had done the right thing after all. There was many a time when we wished we could return to the days when the answer to the question "Where's Jamie?" was always "Wherever you left him."

Chapter 8: Unasseptable Behaviour

With the first year behind us, Jamie started to change - he started to develop personality. He was no longer a baby but a young human being. Meg and I started to get a little more sleep each night too, meaning that we also started to feel a little more like human beings.

We watched him curiously, eager to see what sort of human being he was going to be.

By the time he was three or four years old, he was similar in many ways, to other children his age. Just like other boys, he had certain activities that he really enjoyed doing, such as kicking a football around, doing a jigsaw puzzle, or watching TV. I once witnessed him do all three of these things at the same time.

However, from this age onwards, and for the next ten years or so, his favourite activity, the thing that gave him more pleasure than anything else, was annoying his parents. The thing that he loved most was that mix of irritation and exasperation that came into our facial expressions when certain of our buttons were pressed. He just thought it was funny. We tried explaining to him that upsetting mummy and daddy was not funny, but he just looked at us with a bewildered expression on his face. It was the same expression you would get if you tried to explain to a middle-aged man that *Fawlty Towers* was not funny.

He would never go too far. He did not enjoy seeing his parents wild with fury, sobbing uncontrollably, or bleeding heavily. No, he just liked to make us a little bit cross - perhaps a raised voice, or perhaps a sigh accompanied by a gazing into the middle distance and a yearning for the days before we had children.

The first reaction that most people naturally have whenever they see or hear about a child misbehaving in some way, is to blame the parents. Young children learn from their parents, so the poor behaviour is down to them? Of course, I would usually agree with this, but Jamie, with his myriad of conditions, is surely the exception? It was not our fault, was it? The only thing is, now that I really think about it, I wonder if *The Slipper Game* could have played a part?

When Jamie was a toddler, Meg and I invented a game where we hid one of Meg's slippers somewhere in the bedroom, and Jamie had to find it. As soon as he found it, the real fun began, as Jamie would run out of the room carrying the slipper, giggling, and I would chase after him pretending to be cross. His objective was to throw the slipper over the bannister at the top of the stairs, but he usually became helpless with laughter long before he got that far, and I would catch up with him, then repossess the slipper and hide it again. It was our favourite game, and we sometimes played it for an hour at a time; the sound of Jamie's laughter was not something we tired of quickly. We have a home movie of one session of *The Slipper Game* and it is one of my most treasured possessions, but watching it back today, I cannot help but wonder if the game encouraged Jamie to think that making his Daddy cross was a fun thing to do.

We eventually put a stop to The Slipper Game when Jamie started taking things from the bedroom which were not part of the game and throwing them over the bannister – shoes, coffee mugs, Meg's jewellery box…

As he got older, Jamie discovered other, more imaginative ways of annoying his mum and dad:

- If it was dark outside - turning the lights off.
- If it was light outside - turning the lights on.
- Smashing the light bulbs.
- Knocking the cup out of your hand as you try to drink from it. This works best with scalding hot drinks.
- Throwing the television remote control over the fence into next door's garden.
- Making you think he was about to kiss you on the cheek, but licking you down the side of your face instead.

- Lowering the toilet lid at the most inconvenient moment.

- Loudly calling his parents "gran and granddad" instead of "mum and dad", in public.

- Ensuring his parents have a smear of toothpaste spit on their sleeves at all times.

- Rearranging all the books on the bookshelves into a big pile in the middle of the floor. We had a lot of books.

- Posting things out of the letterbox onto the street outside. Once when left unattended for a while he created a pile of our belongings a foot deep outside the front door. He only stopped because we caught him (Meg looked out the window and commented that the people walking past our front door seemed to be giving it funny looks), otherwise I think he would have posted literally everything in the house that he could fit through the letter box.

- Throwing mobile phones from bedroom windows.

- Microwaving household objects (I can report that he found the reaction resulting from destroying my Nintendo DS in this way particularly satisfying).

- Running away, especially towards busy traffic or open water (as he knew this would create a better reaction from us than just running towards, say, some daffodils).

I mentioned earlier that a common complaint from parents of children with autism is that they find that their child's anxious and compulsive behaviour is often mistaken for naughtiness. For years we had the opposite problem – we had teachers, doctors, and child psychologists telling us that Jamie's behaviour was due to anxiety caused by the Autistic Spectrum Disorder, and it was beyond his control. It wasn't. He just loved being naughty. Maybe *The Slipper Game* played a part, maybe not? Maybe it was the cocktail of Down's syndrome and autism that made his behaviour so unusual, or maybe it was the ADHD, or maybe it was just the way he was. If being naughty was an Olympic event, Jamie could have represented Great Britain. And do you know, over the years, I came to respect him for that. He had a calling, and he followed it.

When Jamie was about five years old, and his difficult behaviour was fully established, there was another little boy with Down's syndrome called Sam living just around the corner from us. He also had ginger hair (I know what you are thinking, and just stop it - Sam's mother did not even know Max) and so Jamie and Sam were often mistaken for each other in public places. Supermarket cashiers would often be overly friendly with Jamie when it was just him and me out shopping together, and they would chat to me about some conversation they had been having with my wife earlier in the week, only to say "Bye-bye Sam" to Jamie as we were leaving. Then the following week, if I was there with Jamie and Meg, I would see, as I pushed the trolley round, the same cashier looking at Meg in a confused manner, perhaps (or maybe I was imagining this) a little reproachfully.

I have often wondered whether the mistaken identity went both ways. I wondered if Sam's mum used to find that when she took him out to play in the park or the local soft-play area, parents of children she had never seen before would usher their children out of Sam's way, saying to them "Stay away from that little boy." Or perhaps when pushing him round a supermarket in a trolley, she wondered why the staff all seemed to tense up whenever the trolley appeared to put Sam within reach of a display of wine bottles. The concept of an "evil twin" is a familiar one, but as far as I know, this was the first example of a "naughty twin". I think, having never suffered from amnesia or tried to fake my own death, this was the closest our lives ever got to being like a daytime soap opera.

Speaking of TV, it was about this time that the show *Supernanny* started to become popular. I am sure that you remember it, it was a big hit in both the UK and the USA. Each week, British nanny Jo Frost would turn up at the home of some family with out-of-control children, and with her no-nonsense attitude, and her inability to pronounce the word "acceptable", she would sort them all out.

It seemed to me that in most episodes, Jo would "face her biggest challenge yet". However, none of the behaviours I saw in the show were as bad as Jamie's. I was often tempted to write to Supernanny's production company and invite them to pay us a visit. A tiny part of me thought that maybe she could have solved all our problems, but mainly I was thinking of the perverse satisfaction I would get from seeing Jo tearing her hair out and admitting that there was nothing she could do, and that we did indeed have the most difficult child in Britain.

The problem she would have had was that her techniques all assumed that children can be reasoned with. She believed that if children knew that bad behaviour had consequences, then they would behave well. Jamie's young mind did not work that way. It would have been like trying to reason with a Terminator. What Jamie saw as the consequence of his bad behaviour was that his mum and dad got cross, which he thought was absolutely hilarious. To him, it was always worth five minutes on the naughty step.

I know what you are thinking – you are thinking "Don't give him the reaction he wants, dumbass!" Of course, we tried this, we tried staying calm. Jamie however, always knew that we were just pretending not to be furious, and he thought that this was even funnier than when we did show it. He would hold eye contact with you, with the suggestion of a grin on his face that said "Come on, we both know you're livid. Let it out, we will both feel better."

Disciplining Jamie was always difficult. The naughty step did not really faze him, and threats to take away toys were always met with a blank stare. If I had smacked him every time he was naughty, the poor boy would have been black and blue – smacking him did not seem to be the right thing to do at all. We tried the carrot as well as the stick (that's a metaphorical stick, just in case social services are reading), we tried praising the good behaviour and ignoring the bad, we tried everything that all the professionals and childcare experts recommended, but still he misbehaved consistently and spectacularly.

All trips out in public became, in our minds, major events that needed careful planning. However, we found that if we planned ahead carefully we could often minimise the damage he caused. It was the mundane everyday life that was the most difficult.

One of the things I dreaded most each day (twice each day in fact) was having to brush his teeth for him. Jamie however, though it was great fun. He seemed to have invented a little game for himself which was in three parts. The first part was trying to knock the toothpaste off the toothbrush before I put it into his mouth, thereby smearing the neat toothpaste on the carpet, the sofa, his clothes, or my clothes. He seemed to favour smearing it on my clothes a lot, so I am guessing that the scoring system he had in his mind for the game gave extra points for this. The second part of the game was when the toothbrush was in his mouth – he would see how many times he had to slap the toothbrush away before he saw that look in my eye that said "I am really fed up but determined not to show it." Sometimes he actually counted aloud. The third part of the game took place when the actual brushing was finished – Jamie would try to spit the toothpaste foam out, covering as wide an area as possible.

The teeth brushing nightmare was particularly annoying because this was something that I was doing for his own good, and yet still he fought against me. If I had just given up trying, it would have been him who suffered, eventually. But no, that was not an option. Instead I tried everything I could think of to make it go more easily. I tried reasoning, pleading, shouting, whispering; I tried tricking him into speaking so that I could slip the toothbrush into his mouth when he opened it. Nothing worked for long. My most embarrassing failure was the time when I tried to use both hands to restrain him and stop him from grabbing the toothbrush, and then did actually try to brush his teeth by gripping the toothbrush in my own teeth. It seemed like a good idea at the time. Jamie just laughed at me. He was right to do so.

One thing that did occasionally work, was the *The Tooth Brushing Song* from the CBeebies TV channel. Sung to the tune of *The Hokey Cokey* it involves putting the toothbrush in and out, and brushing it all about. Sometimes, if he was in the right mood, he would let me brush his teeth if I sang the song while doing so. It was not quite a perfect system – firstly the song is too short for a decent scrub so you have to repeat a few lines several times. Secondly, and I admit this is entirely my own fault, I once accidentally sang some of the words from The Hokey Cokey by mistake: I sang "…and you turn around" instead of "…do the sides" and now Jamie insists on turning around at that point every time I sing the song, even when I sing the correct words. Thirdly, and this time I do blame CBeebies, the song includes the line "spit the toothpaste out" twice, which means I get spat on every time, twice.

If brushing teeth was difficult, cutting his hair was almost impossible. When it came to haircutting he actually was very anxious – it was not naughtiness this time, he really was afraid of the scissors and the clippers. As soon as you approached him with either he started to headbang like a Motörhead fan in a mosh pit.

What were we to do? Were we to let him grow his hair like a ginger version of Cousin It?   It got so bad I once contemplated using hair removal cream on his head. At least we now knew why so many kids with Down's syndrome that I saw on the front of NHS leaflets had such bad haircuts.

And as for the visits to the dentist, I cannot even bring myself to think about them.

One day, I came home from work, and Meg told me that a young mother we were acquainted with had had a nervous breakdown, caused by the stress of motherhood. It seemed surprising to us that somebody with a normal baby could be struggling so badly. We had a conversation about it that went something like this:

Steve: One of us should have a nervous breakdown!

Meg: I haven't got time.

Steve: I mean you should have a tactical nervous breakdown. Have a bit of a rest!

Meg: What would I have to do?

Steve: I'm not sure. What is a "nervous breakdown"? It sounds as though your central nervous system breaks down, which would mean that you just have to lie very still, probably.

Meg: That doesn't sound right.

Steve: Maybe try sobbing lots?

Meg: How long for?

Steve: Maybe a few days?

Meg: And who would look after Jamie?

Steve: Well … me, I guess.

Meg: I think I'll just soldier on, if that's okay.

Whenever I came home from work I used to turn the
final corner onto our driveway with a sense of
trepidation. More often than not the driveway would
be full of things that Jamie had thrown over the
fence: toys, broken pottery, electronic equipment, the
washing, and (during the season) apples and pears
from the trees in the garden. I would spend the first
ten minutes of my evening tidying up and fixing
things, before going into the house to see what havoc
he had wrought in there.

One time the 34" television was broken and lying
forlornly in the middle of the living room floor.
Another time Jamie had broken the lock on the front
door by repeatedly slamming it, so that we could not
leave the house until we got a locksmith out. There
would usually be a new hole in a wall somewhere, or
some broken furniture. I would often come home to
find Meg cleaning up one mess Jamie had made, while

he was off making another mess in another part of the house. That was his preferred tactic – create a diversion with a minor misdemeanour so that he could get up to the real mischief uninterrupted.

Eventually, through trial and error, we learned ways to contain most of the extremes of Jamie's behaviour. We learned how to stay out of his range when holding something fragile or spillable. We learned to hide things from him that we did not want to lose. We learned that if he yelled "SURPRISE!" it meant he was about to do something unspeakable. We had locks fitted on the internal doors of our home so that we could keep him out of certain rooms. We replaced light bulbs and put them in shatterproof protective housings. We strapped Jamie into a wheelchair when we took him on trips out (don't worry, he liked it) so as to stop him running off. I took up running in order to stay fit enough to chase after him in case he ever did get away.

Meg and I turned ourselves into elite commando-style child-care operatives. Whenever we entered a room full of people with Jamie, we both knew within seconds where all the exits were, who was wearing glasses, and which little girls were likely to be targeted for a CUDDLE!

We also found ways to tone down his behaviour a tiny bit, by keeping him calm and giving him a routine. We found we could occasionally get him to do what we asked if he knew something nice was going to happen afterwards. For example - "Please get dressed Jamie, then we will go to the park."

Despite this, looking back, I sometimes think we missed an opportunity in not being on Supernanny. It might have been fun, and it might have helped us. I would have thought that I could have written an interesting enough letter to the producers to get their attention, but I wonder if they would have selected us. We genuinely would have been her toughest challenge yet. Perhaps we would have been too tough – perhaps, like Rocky's opponents at the beginning of Rocky III, the naughty children on the show were all "hand-picked" because the producers knew that Jo could tame them. Perhaps Jamie, as the Clubber Lang of naughty children, would never have got his shot. In the end, the thing that stopped me writing to them though, was the humiliating thought of everyone I had ever met before watching me on TV being run ragged by a five year old.

Chapter 9: Making Waves

Apparently, if you just throw a young baby into the water, it can swim. Apparently they have a natural instinct for it. I checked it on the internet, so it must be true.

It is probably not true. Please do not try it.

You might be worrying at this point that I found out that it is not true the hard way, and that I am about to tell you a "funny" anecdote that involves Jamie nearly drowning. Well, you can relax, I am not going to do that. When Jamie was a baby though, somebody did once try to persuade me that the thing about swimming new-borns was true. He was a big Nirvana fan. We never tested the theory of course; why would we? On the contrary, the first time we took Jamie swimming, when he was just a few months old, he was fully kitted up with a rubber ring <u>and</u> arm bands. Belt and braces, if you like.

We were lucky enough to have a decent swimming pool just a short drive away, and Meg and I (or sometimes just me) took him there as often as we could. Taking Jamie swimming was always great fun.

However, as you might have guessed, our many trips over the years were not entirely without incident. I know that you enjoy hearing about these incidents, otherwise you would have stopped reading after the collection of library stories in the first chapter. The swimming pool has given Jamie many opportunities to misbehave over the years – possibly even more so than the library. There has been more public embarrassment for me at the pool over the years too; at least in the library when Jamie misbehaved I was not stood almost naked and dripping wet while a teenager blew a whistle at me.

There was one incident that comes to mind, which was more shaming and stressful than any of the times at the library. The occasion I am thinking of would have made the time I was lying on the library floor (with Jamie on top of me, hurling Penguin Classics around the room) seem like a happy memory in comparison. I will save that story until the end of the chapter though.

In the early days, Meg, Jamie, and I spent all our time in the learner pool. (We called it the "baby pool". Everyone calls it that don't they? I don't think it is just me.) Jamie was so happy in the water, and the look of determination on his little face as he tried to master his new environment was priceless.

As he got a little older, with the aid of the arm bands, he started to be able to move himself around to wherever he wanted to go. Invariably, wherever he wanted to go would be somewhere Meg and I did not want him to go. Usually, it was in the direction of a total stranger. He would launch himself at them, and throw his arms around them, grinning. If the stranger was a parent, this was usually okay, in fact most of them seemed to quite enjoy it. However, if it was a baby, it was rather more problematic, and had to be followed up by apologies from us, and ushering Jamie away to a quieter part of the pool.

As soon as Jamie got big enough to reach the bottom of the baby pool with his feet, there was no stopping him. He would stride around the pool, waiting for Meg and me to become distracted just long enough for him to make a break for it, and show somebody new some affection. So, we stopped using the baby pool, and graduated to the main pool (or "big pool"? Yes?).

The main thing that the big pool had that the baby pool did not, apart from being bigger (and colder. Grrr!) was that it had a water slide. It was one of those long tubes that began at the top of a wooden staircase and took you outside the building, twisting and turning, before dumping you in the shallow end. Jamie loved it.

When he was very small, I would take him down the slide on my knee. He would shout and giggle all the way down, until the big splash at the end. As soon as he surfaced, he would shout "AGAIN! AGAIN!" So we would do it again, and again.

When he became bigger, he still went down the slide on my knee. It seemed like the only option. Despite the fact that by this point he was actually able to swim a little (doggy paddle – he just seemed to work out how to do it himself one day), sending him down the slide on his own seemed a little risky.

One day though, we decided we had put it off for long enough. By this time he was as tall as Meg, and I could see the lifeguards were looking at us and thinking about saying something, so we decided it was time. Meg waited at the bottom of the slide, and I took Jamie up the staircase to where the lifeguard was waiting at the top, supervising.

I remember they were all very nice lifeguards at the pool. For some reason I once had it in my head that pool lifeguards were cut from the same cloth as nightclub bouncers and traffic wardens, but that is not the case. They were always very sweet young men and women, and I got on well with them even though our relationships were always hampered by me being constantly aware that they were fully dressed and I was just in trunks. None of them had ever complained over the years when Jamie snatched their personal belongings and threw them down the slide (twice it was a drink bottle, one time it was a pair of shoes). Despite what I said earlier, none of them ever blew a whistle at me – I made that up for comic effect. Sorry, I won't do it again.

Anyway, the day that we decided to send Jamie down the slide on his own, their patience was tested more than usual. At the top of the staircase, Jamie and I reached the front of the queue. The lifeguard, gripping his water bottle firmly, gave us the green light, and I sat Jamie at the top of the slide and gave him a little shove. He soon disappeared out of sight, and I heard a "WHEEEEE!"

I turned around and began to walk back down the steps, giving a thumbs up to Meg. Now normally, the ride would last no longer than thirty seconds, but when I reached Meg at the bottom of the slide, a full minute later, Jamie had still not emerged.

"I can hear him." she said.

I listened, and sure enough, over the sound of the water gushing from the slide, I could hear shouting and giggling echoing above me. I peered up into the shadows of the fiberglass tunnel. I could see as far as the final bend; at first I saw nothing, but then I saw Jamie's face peering round the plastic. He saw me and grinned, then disappeared again. He had managed to stand up in the slide, and was swaggering about in there without a care in the world.

By this time the lifeguards had noticed that something was wrong, but seemed to be looking to me to handle it. I shouted up the slide telling Jamie to come down at once, but that was just met with more distant shouting and giggling. Then I heard a stomping noise, and the slide started to shake ominously. Jamie was stamping his feet, and the lifeguards were starting to look concerned. I yelled up the slide some more, but there was nothing I could do, and Jamie knew it.

Eventually, after about five minutes, Jamie's face reappeared at the bend. This time the rest of his body followed him. He stood in the middle of the tunnel and waved at me. I beckoned him down, trying not to look cross, but he knew I was, and he grinned.

I noticed that by now a long queue had built up on the staircase for the slide, and everybody had turned to watch me and Meg. In fact, I think everyone in the pool was watching us.

After another minute or so, Jamie decided he had teased us enough, and he marched down the slide before jumping off the end into my arms.

The lifeguards all visibly relaxed and started to turn away, when Jamie laughed one more time, and shouted "AGAIN!"

I felt several pairs of eyes turn to look at me again, to see how I was going to handle it. I thought for a second, then said loudly, for the lifeguards' benefit, "Okay Jamie. You can go on my knee this time."

That was not the really embarrassing story by the way. I am still working up to that.

Embarrassing incidents do seem to be very common in swimming pools. I once saw a small boy stood by the side of the pool, peeing into the shallow end because his mother, in reply to a request to take him to the toilet, had whispered to him "Just go in the water."

My sister once told me that, while pregnant, she had thrown up in the water.

My old friend Max claims that his swimming trunks once came off as he dived into the water, and a couple of kids stole them. However, Max is a notorious liar, and as this incident is remarkably similar to something that happened on "Mr Bean", I suspect it did not really happen.

Let me now tell you my most embarrassing story. It did not happen in the pool itself, it happened in the changing room.

Jamie was ten years old, and I had been taking him swimming regularly for many years by then, so I had a pretty good routine for getting changed that effectively minimized the likelihood that he would damage something, or escape and get into the pool and cause himself or someone else to drown.

These were the steps to my routine:

1. Get changed together in the group changing room (key provided by pool staff especially for disabled customers).
2. Exit the group changing room and lock door with the key.
3. Hold Jamie's hand while I put the key and all our clothes and valuables in the locker next to the group changing room.
4. Lead Jamie to the toilet.
5. Go in the cubicle with him while he uses the loo.
6. Quick shower for both of us.
7. Go swimming.

On the ill-fated swimming trip in question, steps 1 and 2 went according to plan, but at step 3 there was an unexpected problem. I put all our belongings in the locker, and put the pound coin in the slot, then turned the key to lock it, and nothing happened. The locker had taken my money and refused to lock. So there I was, wearing swimming trunks, trying to control an increasingly impatient child with one hand and trying to fix a broken lock with the other hand. When I realised I could not fix it (due to a complete lack of any skills relevant to lock-fixing), I had a dilemma; I had to go and look for a member of staff to help me which meant I would either have to leave my valuables in the unlocked locker, or unpack the locker and take everything with me which would make holding onto Jamie more or less impossible.

As I stood there, paralyzed with indecision, Jamie made the decision for me, pulling free of my grip and running off towards the toilets; I saw him go inside a cubicle and lock the door. Thinking that he would probably be fine for a few moments, but conscious of the fact that step 5 (above) states that Jamie should be supervised in the toilet cubicle, I ran off to find help and soon returned with capable-looking member of staff who had a screwdriver. While he set about fixing the locker, I tried to coax Jamie out from the toilet cubicle.

I had thought that the worst-case scenario was that Jamie would either refuse to come out of the cubicle, or that perhaps while he was in there he would flush all the toilet paper down the loo; but no, he managed to surprise me with something much worse. When he eventually came out of the cubicle, he was holding his hands in front of him, fingers spread out, and they appeared to be covered in melted chocolate. I was confused. Where could he have got chocolate from? Then, the full horror dawned on me. It was not chocolate.

Quickly, I grabbed Jamie by both elbows, and led him towards the sink at the back of the room.   I turned to the helpful staff member, who was staring with his mouth open at the brown stains all over the cubicle walls, and muttered "Sorry mate, I think you're going to have to give that a bit of a wipe down." When I reached the sink and started washing Jamie, he did not resist, thank goodness; if he had decided to struggle against me...well, I cannot bear to think about it. I am not sure why Jamie did what he did. It did not seem to be a deliberate attempt to be naughty, and he seemed just as surprised by the results as the rest of us.

While all this was going on, another member of staff came in from the pool side, looking for me and Jamie. Meg, who had by now got changed in the ladies' changing room and was in the pool, had been wondering where I was, so had sent a lifeguard in to the men's changing room to check her husband and son were okay. I indicated to him, perhaps unconvincingly given the circumstances, that all was well. I imagined him going back to her and saying "Is your son four feet tall, with Down's syndrome and ginger hair, and covered in poo? If so, he is fine."

Eventually, after a thorough scrub, and another apology to another appalled-but-trying-not-to-show-it member of staff who had to clean up the sink area, we progressed to step 6, the shower, (and I thought it prudent to have a longer shower than originally scheduled), and eventually step 7. Swimming. At last.

As I made my way out towards the pool I avoided making eye contact with the poor guys who were cleaning up Jamie's mess. Half of me was feeling sorry for them, the other half was thinking "This is nothing, you guys only have to deal with this today; this is my life!" The other half (well, you know what I mean) was thinking that if their lockers had been working properly, none of this shit would have happened in the first place.

Chapter 10: Exile on Mainstream

On the advice of our social worker, in order to "improve his social skills", we signed Jamie up for a mainstream nursery which was attached to the local primary school.

Within a few days he had charmed all the adults there with his cheeky grin and warm personality. The children, however, were another story; he just did not seem to like them being around him very much and was not shy about letting them know. After a few incidents of spitting and hair pulling, the other children seemed to get the message, and started giving him a wide berth. The Wendy House (with sub post office) became Jamie's territory, and the other children stayed away. Jamie seemed to like it that way, but we rather felt that this defeated the object of taking him to nursery. His social skills were not improving. On the other hand though, Meg now had two whole hours each day to herself. So we decided to carry on with it.

Jamie was the only child there with special needs. The other parents were all very polite and pleasant to us at the drop-offs and pick-ups, but none of them seemed to know exactly how to talk to us. The usual rules of small-talk seemed not to apply, and I think we made them feel slightly uncomfortable.

The staff were a lot easier with us. When they found out that there was a child with special needs attending their nursery, they really embraced the opportunity to try to make a difference in his life, and I found that touching. I like to imagine them organising a meeting to discuss what they could do – possibly using a flipchart and marker pens, and maybe bandying around phrases like "brainstorming" and "blue sky thinking" (although that perhaps says more about my background in the corporate world than it does about them). Anyway, the big idea that they came up with was to send a few of the staff on a course to learn Makaton.

Makaton, in case you don't know, is a sign language (and it also sometimes incorporates picture symbols). It is often used with individuals who cannot speak and also have some other cognitive impairment such as Down's syndrome or autistic spectrum disorder (or both!). It is also commonly used with stroke patients. Makaton was invented in the 1970s by a speech therapist called Margaret Walker, and her assistants Katharine Johnston and Tony Cornforth. The main idea is that it is a simple sign language, and unlike most other sign languages, the signs usually have a visual relationship with the word they are referring to – they are almost a mime. For example, the Makaton sign for dinner is to mime putting food into your mouth, and the sign for a book is the same as it would be if you were playing charades.

Meg and I first came across Makaton when someone gave us an old video to watch (for any kids reading this, a video is what streaming was called in Victorian times). The video starred children's TV presenter Dave Benson Phillips, and featured him reciting nursery rhymes for an hour, in exotic locations like parks, and streets, signing in Makaton as he went along. As unpromising as this sounds, Jamie loved it. He would watch the video over and over. These were the days when Jamie was a very demanding toddler, and it was before CBeebies existed, so getting Jamie to watch TV for an hour instead of insisting that we entertain him was quite some respite for us. I promised myself that if I ever met Dave Benson Phillips I would thank him and shake his hand (As it happens, I did meet him, about ten years later, and I did thank him and I did shake his hand. He was very nice, but I could tell he had no idea what I was talking about).

After speaking to a few speech and play therapists, Meg decided to learn Makaton for herself. Her mum, who knew it through her work in special care, helped her. Before long, Meg knew all the main signs and could converse in the language pretty fluently. I decided to learn it too; it did not come as naturally to me as it did to Meg, but I did try. I watched that Dave Benson Phillips video again and again, and picked up a lot of the signs, but I found this was not really enough to have a conversation, as I only knew the words that were present in nursery rhymes. If ever I meet a stroke patient who wants to chat about the oranges and lemons he saw while row row rowing his boat round and round the garden, I know I will be okay; if he is trying to ask me for advice on what the best mobile-phone contract is though, I will be no use to him.

Jamie did learn a few signs that helped him communicate. He used signs to ask for his dinner, the toilet, or a drink of milk ("milk" is my favourite Makaton sign – you have to mime milking the udders of a tiny cow).

So anyway, we were very pleased to learn that the nursery teachers were using Makaton. It came as a bit of a surprise to us - we did not know anything about it until one morning when Meg decided to go into the nursery and help out. She occasionally used to do that – she said it was nice to see Jamie with other children, but without feeling the pressure of the responsibility of looking after him. On this occasion Angela, one of the teachers, had decided to lead the class in a sing-song, and the song she chose was Twinkle Twinkle Little Star. Meg was delighted to see that Angela had learned the Makaton signs for all the words, and was signing along as she was singing. The children all watched with interest, and a few of them joined in, copying the "actions". The only problem was that Meg, as a more experienced signer, noticed that one of the signs was not quite correct. At the end of the session, she quietly took Angela aside to point this out.

Meg: "Your signing was very good."

Angela: "Thank you."

Meg: "There is just one little thing – I hope you don't mind me saying - the sign for star is actually this." [demonstrates the correct sign for a star]

Angela: "Oh really. I thought it was this." [demonstrates the same sign she did during the song, forming a diamond shape with her hands.]

Meg: "No...er..." [laughs nervously] "that means something quite different actually."

Angela: "What does it mean?"

Meg: "Er... it means vagina."

Angela: [stunned silence]

Both:	[awkward pause]
Angela:	"So I was actually signing ... Twinkle Twinkle Little Vagina?"
	[Another pause as Angela tries to take in what she had just been told]
Meg:	"I am sure nobody noticed."

Well, nobody did notice, apart from the wife of the man who thought it was hilarious and made a mental note that if ever he wrote a book about his experiences, it would definitely be going in. Sorry Angela.

Apart from being encouraged to sing songs about twinkling genitals, Jamie got on relatively well at the nursery. We were told about one minor problem, that apparently Jamie was in the habit of grabbing other people's shoes whenever they took them off, then running off with them, laughing, and throwing them over the little balcony at the end of the room. One of the teachers asked me if I knew why he did this, and I just shrugged, shuffled my feet, and muttered something about sensory overloading, before changing the subject.

There was one unpleasant incident I should probably mention. It happened on another of Meg's visits. According to her, she was playing with some of the other children when she became aware that one of the teachers was looking for one of the little boys, Mackenzie. Mackenzie was a sweet-natured little boy with beautiful curly blonde hair. He had not been seen for a minute or two, so the teacher was calling out his name. After a few seconds there was a grunt from inside the Wendy House, and the door was shoved open. Jamie staggered out, dragging Mackenzie along the floor behind him, by the hair. "Here he is!" said Jamie (it may have actually just been his body language that said it, as he was not really speaking by then, but it was definitely what he meant). To Jamie's bemusement, the grown-ups did not seem pleased that he had found Mackenzie for them. Mackenzie was sobbing. Jamie looked down at the fistful of blonde hair he was holding and seemed to be wondering how it had come out.

Mackenzie's mother was informed of the incident when she came to pick him up later on (I don't think that not informing her was ever an option, given the bald patch on the top of Mackenzie's head) and Meg was worried there was going to be quite a scene. The mother though, just took one look at Jamie, and shrugged it off – "No real harm done."

I am sure that not every mother would have taken that approach, but we were very grateful that she did.

I am sure there were a few more incidents that happened on days Meg was not there, but generally, we were given the impression that Jamie was doing okay. Developmentally, he was clearly well behind the other children his age, but he was still within sight of them. A few of the teachers got quite enthusiastic about his abilities. One of them even told us that she thought Jamie was "gifted" at maths. As far as I can gather, she came to this conclusion because of his fascination with the children's TV show "Numberjacks", which featured anthropomorphised integers who combated the forces of evil by harnessing the awesome power of basic arithmetic. I think Jamie just liked the colours.

With all the encouragement we got from the nursery school teachers, we began to allow ourselves to believe that if we could just give Jamie a little more support, perhaps he could catch the other children up. So we put in the extra effort. Meg in particular worked tirelessly in the afternoons while I was at work, trying to interest him in reading, speech, and numbers. He fought against us though, and it was a battle we were never going to win, but I am glad we tried.

Towards the end of that year, while we were deciding which school to send Jamie to, the subject of "Special Schools" kept cropping up in the news; politicians seemed to be suggesting that it was better for disabled children to attend mainstream schools rather than schools that were exclusively for disabled children. Looking back, it seems unbelievable now, but we allowed ourselves to be talked into enrolling Jamie into the local mainstream primary school. Jamie was given a statement of special educational needs, and the school recruited a classroom assistant especially for him - a "one to one" whose sole responsibility was looking after him. Or, as it turned out, protecting other people from him.

So we bought Jamie a school uniform, complete with little grey short trousers, and we had him measured for smart school shoes (That was fun. I don't think the assistant in that shoe shop will ever forget him!), and on his first day of school we took him in to his new classroom. It was a curious experience – the first day of school is always strange day for any parent. Looking around us at the other parents, there was a clear distinction between the first-time parents who were nervously asking the teacher a lot of questions, and the older parents who had seen it all before, laughing and joking as they dropped off their second or third child (in one case, tenth). None of the other parents were in our position though – none of the other children were like Jamie.

We met the one-to-one, Rita. She was young but she seemed confident. Reluctantly, we kissed Jamie goodbye, and left him with Rita, wishing her luck.

The first day did not go terribly well. Rita looked a little fraught as she handed him back to us, but she was trying to put on a brave face. On the second day,

Jamie upset some of the other children. I never found out what he did, but I got some stern looks from other parents at pick-up time. On the third day he bit his teacher.

I am not going to try to blame the teacher. I like school teachers. I think the reason most have them chose their profession in the first place was that they genuinely want to help children to fulfil their potential and make the world a better place. People often accuse teachers of choosing the career because they liked the sound of the long holidays, or because they liked the idea of being able to boss kids around all day. There might be a few individuals that does apply to (I am thinking here of a particular PE teacher from a northern grammar school in the 1980s. Let's call him Mr Smith shall we? That was actually his name), but I think those people are a lot rarer than a lot of folk seem to think.

Despite the best efforts of Jamie's teacher, it was obvious that it was not going to work. The classrooms were too small to allow Jamie to go off and be on his own. In reception class there was very little structure, but even the little that there was was too much for him. If he could not cope with that there was no way he was going to be able to manage the formality required for lessons in later years.

So what were we going to do? We had no idea what our options were.

On the fourth day, I came home from work to find Meg in an excited mood. A social worker had been out to visit her and told her about the Milestone, a school for children with special needs that was just a twenty minute drive away in Gloucester. Keen to find out more, Meg had been to visit it, and had been astonished at what she had seen. It was a modern, purpose-built special school, with amazing facilities, full of dedicated and professional staff, and happy children.

Less than a week after starting at the mainstream school, we switched to the Milestone.

Chapter 11: Special School Days

It was Meg who took Jamie to school for his second first day. She told me afterwards that it was quite an overwhelming experience for her, that it was "full-on special needs". As she walked Jamie through the school to his new classroom there were all sorts of children milling about; some were in wheelchairs, some had Down's syndrome, some had cerebral palsy, and one was wearing a blue helmet for some reason that was not immediately obvious to either of us. She noticed that the place was looking a little tired, and that toys lying around looked quite worn out.

She overheard two parents talking in a corridor, being competitive about how disabled their children were:

"I didn't get a wink of sleep last night. Charlie was up all night with an anxiety attack."

"You're lucky, we had to blue light Nathan to Gloucester Hospital because he stopped breathing!"

Just as she was thinking of turning around and taking Jamie home again, his new teacher Bev appeared, and greeted them both so warmly that she found herself smiling back, and leading Jamie into the classroom. Her biggest worry, that Jamie would not be able to communicate with the teachers, evaporated when the classroom assistants all welcomed Jamie using Makaton, saying hello and asking him if he wanted a drink, or to go to the toilet.

The teacher was happy for Meg to stay with Jamie for as long as she wanted to, and that ended up being all day. She went back again the next day too.

If you have never been inside a special school then your opinion of them is probably wrong. Before I actually went to see one, I assumed that they were grim establishments akin to mental institutions. I visualised dark corridors with screams heard in the distance, and a stern headmistress who you suspect would melt if you threw a bucket of water over her. They are actually really life-affirming places full of happy and positive people.

If you ask a teacher at a special school (and I did ask one, so I can say this with confidence) what it is that makes the special school different from a regular one, he/she will say that the main difference is that they practise pupil-centred learning. That is, the teaching style is adapted according to each pupil's interests, abilities, and learning styles. For us, and for Jamie, this was crucial; Jamie was never going to learn anything in a traditional classroom environment. There would be no point in trying to follow the national curriculum – even if he could have been motivated to take an interest in photosynthesis, I don't think there is a Makaton sign for it.

The special schools also have better facilities than regular schools for dealing with disabled children. The Milestone has full time school nurses, physiotherapists, and speech therapists. Smaller class sizes too, and the classes are run by teachers who are specially trained.

Despite all this, it seems that special schools in the UK have been under pressure in recent years, simply because there are now more children with special needs. This is largely due to medical intervention – babies are being saved that previously would have died, and they soon grow up, often with disabilities. There has also been a recent increase in disabilities caused by the mother using drugs or alcohol during pregnancy. Teachers at the Milestone have also said that the behaviour associated with autistic spectrum disorder seems to be getting more extreme, and that there has been an increase in children with overlapping conditions, such as autistic spectrum disorder and Down's syndrome, like Jamie.

Even though the teachers at the Milestone were highly trained, and they were experienced in teaching some of the most difficult children imaginable, Jamie was still quite a challenge for them. I was once told that Jamie had "a reputation" among the staff for being unpredictable and difficult. However, I was also told that as soon as any teacher actually got to know him, their opinion would change, and they would love him.

At the end of every school day the teachers would write us a message in a little notebook, saying how he had got on that day. We noticed that they always tried to put a positive spin on things. If he was naughty they always said he had been "silly", "unsettled" or "agitated". If he was very naughty, they might say "uncooperative". If he had rampaged around the school destroying the fabric of the building, they would say he had "exhibited challenging behaviour". At least, that is what I assumed.

Although Jamie was not capable of telling us directly about what he got up to at school, he did give us a bit of an insight into his life by doing impressions. Alone in his bedroom he would often act out scenes from his day, sometimes using his toys, sometimes just by talking to himself. We would often hear him shouting at the top of his voice, in what we assumed were impersonations of his teachers:

"OH NO! DON'T DO THAT!"

"LOOK! IT'S BROKEN"

"THAT'S NOT FUNNY!"

"OH, JAMIE!"

"OH MY GOD!"

For that last one he would always adopt an accent uncannily like a particular young classroom assistant that we knew.

At parents' evening we were told about the work that he did every day, learning about things like brushing teeth, taking turns, and road safety, as well as the basics of reading and writing and arithmetic. We also got to hear in detail of the funny things that Jamie had done. It was obvious that the teachers had a lot of affection for him, and enjoyed telling us about his exploits. Over the years we got to hear many stories of the times he had caused trouble, but these stories were always told to us with a smile.

At first Jamie used to try to escape from the classroom. Whenever the classroom door was opened, he would attempt to run for it. Once free he would sprint off down the corridors, giggling, with teachers and classroom assistants in hot pursuit. The teachers soon cottoned on to this, and began to keep an especially close eye on him.

The door to the classroom was no ordinary door - it was specially designed to stop children like Jamie from escaping. It had two handles that had to be turned at the same time - one was at waist height, the other at head height. This way, a child could not open it, not being able to reach the top handle. Well, not unless the child stood on a chair, reached up to the top handle, and used his foot to turn the bottom handle. It took Jamie about five minutes to figure that out. I saw him do it once at a parents' evening. He had been sitting quietly at a table, doing some colouring while I chatted to the teacher, when for no apparent reason he threw a box of pens across the room, scattering them everywhere. While the teacher and I were distracted picking them up, he whipped the chair out, stood on it to open the door, and was off down the corridor before the teacher and I knew anything about it.

During the school day Jamie had to be watched at all times, and laminated notices also went up around the school warning all staff and visitors to keep the doors leading out into the street closed, as one of the children was "a runner".

One of Jamie's most audacious classroom escape bids happened when a maintenance man came to fix one of the locks on the door. In silence, Jamie watched the man take apart some of the mechanism of the door handle, and the teachers allowed him to watch because he seemed so interested in what was quite a complex task. Eventually, the job completed, the maintenance man went to tell the teacher he was finished. As he was packing up, he discovered that he was missing a screwdriver. A little worried, the teacher and classroom assistants all stopped what they were doing, and began to search the room for it, looking under chairs and tables, in books, and everywhere they could think of. Eventually, one of them looked up and saw Jamie with the screwdriver in his hand. Making the most of the staff's distraction, he was attempting to unscrew the door handle.

As the years went by, Jamie's desire to experience more of the world immediately outside his window seemed to wane a little. He stopped trying to get out of the door, and he stopped trying to run off whenever he was taken outside the classroom. Eventually, one of his teachers decided to embark on a bold experiment. Every morning, when the teacher had taken registration, one of the children was asked to carry the register to the school secretary. Jamie of course, had never been asked to do this, but that was about to change. The teacher recognized that Jamie was more mature now, and it was time to trust him with his freedom. It transpired that the teacher was right to trust him - Jamie took the register to the secretary and returned to his classroom straight away. For the first few days that this happened, there were members of staff positioned en route, casually keeping an eye on him; eventually though he was trusted to do the job himself without supervision.

Almost every time, Jamie delivered his package and returned to his classroom immediately. On one occasion though, temptation did get the better of him. On his way back to the classroom Jamie spotted a Henry Hoover that had been left in the corridor, and he plugged it in and started using it. There happened to be a visitor to the school that day who was being given a guided tour by one of the staff. Both visitor and staff member were surprised to turn a corner and see a small boy with Down's syndrome vacuuming in the corridor with a look of concentration on his face.

Taking the register to the secretary was a popular job among the children, because the secretary often gave a boiled sweet to the child who brought it to her. As Jamie did not like boiled sweets though, he usually took it back to the classroom and gave it to another child instead. One day however, when he got back to the classroom, he presented the sweet to the teacher for a change. Feeling flattered at the honour bestowed upon her, the teacher smiled and popped it into her mouth. It took a split second for the horrible truth to register in her mind - the sweet was wet. Jamie had sucked it, spat it out, rewrapped it and given it away. It seems quite likely that he had been doing this for weeks, without any of the other children complaining. After that day, the sweets stopped.

When Jamie was nine he was actually invited to go on a residential trip with his class, to a place called Macaroni Woods. There, the teachers took the children for walks, and did all sorts of outdoor activities. At home, Meg and I had a nice evening off from looking after him; it was a strange sensation, we both felt as though we had forgotten something all evening. I would like to be able to tell you that we used our night off to go out clubbing, or for a hot air balloon ride, or something exciting, but I think we just stayed in and watched *Lost*. When Jamie got back the next day, his teacher Jayne told us that he had had a lovely time, and had been well behaved, if a little excitable. Years later though, Jayne told me the truth, that she had not actually slept a wink that night as Jamie spent the whole night leaping around the mattresses and talking at a hundred miles an hour, pausing only for a five minute power-nap (taken while sitting up) every now and then.

On one of my more recent visits to the school a teacher pointed out to me that they had had a bolt fitted on the outside of the door of the staff toilet, at the top, so that it could be locked from the outside. I was told that the reason for this is that Jamie often walked past this door, and had taken to running inside and locking himself in. Of course there is a mechanism for unlocking the door from the outside, but it doesn't work if someone on the inside is gripping the lock still firmly with his fingers. Apparently he could keep this up for fifteen minutes. So now they use the bolt to lock the door to stop Jamie from going in, but they are also aware of a new risk, that if Jamie could stand on a chair or table and reach the bolt, he could lock someone inside the toilet. I could tell from the look in the teacher's eye that she knew it was just a matter of time.

One facility the school offered which made our lives a lot easier, was the school bus service. Every day Jamie was picked up from our home by either a minibus or a taxi. In theory it was supposed to be the same driver and chaperone team every day, but in practice we found that they would often change after a few months. There was a cycle that repeated itself time after time. A cheerful new driver would turn up at our house and take Jamie away, then in the afternoon he would bring him back, joking that he was "a bit of a handful". Over the next few weeks the joking would stop, and we would hear whispers of complaints being made, refusal to work in dangerous conditions, and eventually a cheerful new driver would turn up one day (much to Jamie's delight, as he knew that meant he had broken another one).

One chaperone (still in her early days with us when it all seemed funny) told us in reply to the question "Has he been well-behaved today?" that Jamie had, at one point, taken all his clothes off and ran around the bus naked, but other than that he had been fine.

I am sure that I could get an entire chapter out of the stories that drivers and chaperones could tell me about Jamie. I cannot interview any of them though, because strangely, after working with Jamie, they don't seem to want to keep in touch with us, and many seem to have retired from working with children with special needs.

There have been a few drivers and chaperones over the years who Jamie did not break. There was a friendly Geordie woman called Chris who seemed to have genuine affection for him (and he liked her too – perhaps the accent reminded him of his grandparents). The pair who put up with the most though, was Sharon and Evita, who survived everything Jamie could throw at them. I mean that literally; he would throw things at Sharon while she was driving the minibus - shoes mostly. One of the previous drivers had once threatened to quit because Jamie threw a tissue at her, but Sharon did not threaten to quit, she just took Jamie's shoes off him when the bus was in motion. Evita, the chaperone, has also had to put up with being slapped and kicked a lot (although the kicking was not as bad once his shoes were removed). We know this was a sign of affection, as he liked her very much; he was forever trying to drag her into the house with him at the end of the day.

It was Evita's responsibility to keep him in his seat for the whole journey, a task which despite the use of a "Houdini belt" has not proved easy. Houdini belts are special harnesses that are supposed to be escape-proof, but as Evita would testify, they are not. They are named after Harry Houdini, the famous escapologist, who actually used to dislocate his own shoulder in order to get out his harnesses, then pop it back in again later. We don't think Jamie does that when he escapes, but we don't know how he does do it. Houdini, of course, used his talent to make a fortune for himself and become one of the most famous men in the world, but Jamie just uses his talent to get out of his seat so that he can go and spit at Sharon.

Because we had such a good relationship with some of the teachers, we got to hear a few stories about other children and their families – stories that get told and retold in the staffroom. I am sure Jamie has been the subject of many of these stories himself over the years, but I would like to end this chapter with a story that is not about him, for a change.

A teacher called Kate Bloggs (not really of course, but I was asked to change the name) had a pupil in her class called David. They had an informal relationship, and he always called her "Kate", rather than "Miss Bloggs". One day, a school administrator visited the classroom and had a conversation with the teacher, calling her "Miss Bloggs" several times, which David and the other children overheard. When the administrator left the room, David went up to the

teacher and stared at her with an incredulous
expression on his face.

"That's amazing!" he said eventually. "Miss Bloggs,
you look exactly like my teacher Kate!"

Chapter 12: Down's Syndrome World

Having a child with special needs does make you sensitive to everything you see on the subject in the media.

Whenever the Paralympics comes around, I watch it with more interest than I would otherwise have done. People ask my opinion on it as though I am an authority on the subject, and I often get asked if Jamie might compete in it one day. I always give the same answer, it is not a difficult question – no, he won't. It's not because I have doubts about his athletic prowess, it's because there is not actually a special division for people with Down's syndrome. There is a category for people with learning disabilities, but not specifically Down's syndrome. This means people with Down's syndrome would have to compete against people who were mentally slow but with no physical disabilities at all. (As a joke, I originally named a famous footballer here as an example, but my dad persuaded me I might be causing trouble for myself, so I deleted it. I am sure you can guess who it was going to be though.)

I was surprised to discover that fact a few years ago, when I was looking into the possibility of Jamie getting involved. I believe I have mentioned that he is a fast runner, but he can also throw things, lift things, and swim like a fish (a fish doing doggy paddle that is). I am sure he would be a medal favourite if competing against others with his condition, as long as we could persuade him to actually compete. Unfortunately I can imagine him getting disqualified at the starting line-up for hurling himself at the athlete next to him, demanding a cuddle. Maybe it is just as well that he doesn't have a category. I guess the committee knows what it is doing after all.

The Paralympics is just one example of an event that is far more significant to me than it would otherwise have been. There are many more. News stories, TV dramas, jokes ... things that I might not have even noticed before, let alone had an opinion about, suddenly seem very relevant, often poignant, and sometimes upsetting. I am going to spend this chapter discussing a few of these things. This is not going to be a comprehensive analysis of all things to do with Down's syndrome in the world, just the ones that made an impression on me during Jamie's childhood, and have stayed with me since.

I will begin with movies. I have always been a big movie fan. I grew up living above a video store in the 1980s, and I watched almost every movie that passed through it, over the years. I continued the love affair into adulthood, embracing satellite channel subscriptions, DVD-by-mail, Blu-ray, and now streaming. What I am trying to say is that I have seen a lot of movies. And how many movies have I seen that include prominent characters with Down's syndrome? I can think of five, three of which were foreign language films.

Café de Floret features Vanessa Paradis as the single mother of a little boy with Down's syndrome. At first she seems to be a loving parent, determined to do the best for her son no matter what obstacles are put in front of her. Eventually though, she becomes jealous and bitter. I thought it was a good movie – there are several interesting characters and two very different stories that are woven together skilfully. It is stylish, intriguing, sexy, and suspenseful. But will it make you feel good about Down's syndrome? No.

The movie *The Eighth Day* is a French film in which one of the main characters, played by Pascal Duquenne, has Down's syndrome. I stumbled across it on TV while channel-hopping one evening, not long after Jamie was diagnosed. The film had just started and I thought that it would do me good to watch it. It is a bit like *Rain Man*, but with Down's syndrome instead of autism. A businessman whose life is going down the wrong track learns something about life and about himself, from a disabled companion. Sounds positive and uplifting? Well, it all works out very well for the businessman character, but not so much for the poor young man with Down's syndrome. The ending is very upsetting. I was wrong about it doing me good to watch it.

A far more enjoyable film is the 1991 Belgian movie *Toto the Hero*. It features Pascal Duquenne again, this time in a smaller role. *Toto the Hero* is European in the best way - a tale of passion and tragedy told in a stylish and funny way, with fantasy elements and dreamlike sequences that I cannot imagine seeing in an English language movie. It is not really "about" Down's syndrome as such, it just happens to have a character in it with the condition. I really enjoyed watching it, and was so relieved to finally see a movie that featured Down's syndrome positively.

Of the two English language movies I can think of, *Truly Madly Deeply* is probably the most well-known. It is a sort of British version of *Ghost* but with more Snape and less Swayze, and with more cello playing and less erotic pottery. There are a couple of cringe-worthy scenes with dialogue that made my toes curl up so much I thought they might break, but if you can get past those it is a funny and sweet movie with some interesting ideas behind it. About half way through we meet a new character who works with disabled people. The disabled people in the movie are not really well defined characters, they are just there to let the audience know that the new guy is a decent person. But what the hell, everyone seems to be having a good time, so I will give it the benefit of the doubt and count it as a positive movie.

The other English language movie I can think of is *Notes on a Scandal.* This is a decent drama, well worth watching. Cate Blanchett's character happens to have a son with Down's syndrome, and she clearly loves him very much. Again then, let's call it positive shall we?

A quick search on the internet reveals that, of course, there are a few more that I have not got round to seeing yet, including *The Ringer*, *Coming Down the Mountain*, *Precious*, and a documentary film which is actually called *Up Syndrome* (dammit, when I made that joke in chapter 2, I thought I was the first person ever to think of it). Even so, it does seem that Down's syndrome is underrepresented by the movie industry, especially Hollywood.

Oh, hold on, I have just noticed that *The Ringer* is available for streaming, so I am going to watch it now and get back to you with a review. Don't go away.

Okay, I'm back. It was rubbish.

Let us turn instead to the world of television drama.

In 2006, the British soap opera *EastEnders* featured a storyline where one of the characters, Honey Mitchell (yes, her name really was Honey, I double-checked), had a child with Down's syndrome, Janet.

There was quite a fuss made in the media about this *EastEnders* storyline, when Janet was born, and all the reports I saw and heard praised the show for its sensitivity. I did watch the episode myself though, and I just found the whole thing depressing. There was a particularly troublesome scene just before the relatives found out the diagnosis, where they were stood in a dark room, ominously toasting to the baby's health, wealth, and beauty. It was a great if you were a fan of dramatic irony, but a bit of a downer if you were someone who had recently come to terms with Down's syndrome as not being all that bad after all. It felt as though *EastEnders* was telling me I was wrong to have gotten over it. I decided not to watch the rest of the storyline, which I believed focused on Honey's spiral into despair, before moving away and taking her baby with her. I don't think it would have helped me.

I suppose the argument is that by highlighting the difficulties that parents face, they are raising awareness. I hear people talking all the time about the importance of raising awareness of terrible things like breast cancer, climate change, and sex trafficking, but the thing is, I don't want to think of Down's syndrome as a terrible thing that the public should be warned about. I would much rather see happy and confident individuals with Down's syndrome on TV that show the public it is nothing to be feared.

As it happens, I heard Janet Mitchell reappeared in *Eastenders* a few years later, this time without a general wailing or gnashing of teeth. Perhaps one of the writers does see it the same way that I do after all.

There probably are other British dramas featuring Down's syndrome (I bet Casualty had a few), I am sure I have missed some. But let's move on to America now, shall we? What has their TV output been like?

In the first season of *American Horror Story*, Jessica Laing's character has a teenage daughter with Down's syndrome. The daughter is quite a significant character in the show; she is given her own personality and her own motivation, and is more than just a stereotype. She does get (spoiler alert) brutally murdered after a few episodes, but since just about everybody in the show gets brutally murdered at some point, it felt to me like she achieved equality with the rest of the cast. You go girl!

In *Glee* the only thing that got murdered was the music. I wish I liked *Glee,* but watching it makes me want to superglue my eyelids shut and pour hot wax into my ears. The reason I wish I liked it though, is that it does have the most positive portrayal of Down's syndrome I have ever seen on TV. The gym teacher, Sue Sylvester (who is the only thing I like in the show) has a sister with Down's syndrome, and also appoints a young girl with the condition as a cheerleader. It's all handled surprisingly well, and is both sensitive and funny at the same time, without falling into the trap of being sentimental or patronizing. It's just that music...

So what about the world of comedy then? Could that make me feel better?

Well actually, yes, it can. There's a comedy show on Channel 4 called *The Last Leg* which is fresh and funny, and disability-friendly. It was linked to the Paralympics when it first started in 2012, but has now continued on its own. It developed the idea that you can joke about disabilities, as long as the joke comes from a good place. It focusses mainly on physical disabilities, but not exclusively. One memorable 2014 episode of *The Last Leg* featured a young man with Down's syndrome called James, who was introduced to the audience to explicitly make the point that the world is a better place for having people like him in it. James made the most of his brief appearance, blowing kisses to the camera, and as co-presenter Josh Widdicombe put it, "he didn't half milk that". It was fully milked, and the audience loved it.

The 2006 Ricky Gervais sitcom *Extras* had a storyline where the main character Andy, a minor celebrity, inadvertently offends the family of a child with Down's syndrome. The child was being noisy in a restaurant, and Andy, not realising the child had special needs, complained to the management. The press soon got hold of the story and Andy was branded heartless and unfeeling, and was eventually forced to apologise.

The Inbetweeners sitcom had a similar joke in a 2008 episode, where the main character Will ranted at a group of people he accused of "pushing in" to the front of an amusement park ride, not realising that they had Down's syndrome. When he realised what he had done, he was horrified, and said to himself "I am the worst human being in the world!"

I thought that both jokes were very funny - they were about people's attitudes to disability rather than disability itself, and I found it rather refreshing that Down's syndrome was being acknowledged by comedy rather than just being treated as a totally taboo subject.

Unfortunately though, Ricky Gervais was on the wrong side of a controversy in 2011, which started on the social media website Twitter. New to Twitter at the time, Gervais had been posting pictures of himself pulling faces, and using the word "mong" in captions to describe them.

Eventually, fellow British comedian Richard Herring pointed out on his blog that this was an insensitive thing to do, and would cause offence to disabled people and their families. Gervais argued that the word mong did not mean Down's syndrome any more, in the same way that gay no longer meant happy. He accused Herring of being jealous of his success, and then of merely trying to create publicity for his upcoming tour. Furthermore, Herring found himself on the receiving end of thousands of abusive messages from angry Gervais fans: some accused him of censorship, some were obnoxious ("MONG! MONG! MONG! MONG MONG!") and some just offensive ("Who the hell is Richard Herring? I'd call him a mong, but I don't want to insult mongs!!" a message which, incidentally, rather steps on Gervais's point that mong does not mean Down's syndrome any more).

I don't think Gervais himself was really trying to be offensive; I just think he just had a few moments of thoughtlessness. Comedians these days are generally very clever and thoughtful people, and it seems to me that most of the successful ones are decent people too. None of the top comedians would ever be deliberately nasty about disabled people? Surely?

Well, there was one once - a very successful Scottish comedian who I won't name. According to *The Daily Telegraph* and *The Guardian,* amongst others, the comedian included a lengthy routine in his live show about how "Mongoloids" have a low life expectancy. He also included jokes about their appearance and did impressions of how they talk. The reason the story hit the news was that during one show, the mother of a five year old girl with Down's syndrome confronted him, telling him how upset she was. Actually, I think I will name him after all. If I don't, you might think it was Billy Connolly. It was Frankie Boyle.

I expect you found that last story a bit depressing to read. Imagine how I feel – I had to type it! In my experience of Down's syndrome and disabilities I have encountered so many nice people it has really been quite touching, but I am also aware that we live in a world where certain comedy audiences fall about laughing at nasty jokes about disabled people because, presumably, the comedian is just saying what they are secretly thinking. I don't understand it, but I suppose that given that we know the human race includes paedophiles, war criminals, and northern PE teachers, perhaps I should not be so surprised.

Or is it as simple as that? I have been to comedy gigs where the comedian has said something controversial, and other audience members have found it offensive and walked out, but I have found it funny. I laughed not because I agreed with what the comedian said (I assumed he did not really mean it), but because I enjoyed seeing a talented comic playfully pushing boundaries. I remember thinking that the people who had walked out had just not got the joke.

I did not hear Boyle's jokes about Down's syndrome, so I cannot say for sure what his intention was in telling them. However, I did once hear him make a joke about how he expects that Katie Price's disabled son will grow up and try to rape her one day. There was certainly nothing playful about that joke.

Whatever Boyle's intention, I know that if I had been in the audience that night, I would have been just as upset as the woman in the story. If it feels as though someone is attacking someone you love while everyone else in the room laughs along, it is difficult to see the funny side.

Generally, stories about Down's syndrome in the news are rarely uplifting. A baby with Down's syndrome in Australia was left with her surrogate mother while the biological parents kept the baby's twin, who did not have the condition. Professional atheist Richard Dawkins claimed on Twitter that it would be immoral not to abort a foetus that had been diagnosed with Down's.

There was one story though, that I did find very uplifting in the early days. The first ever series of the British version of the reality TV show *Big Brother* was won by a likeable young builder called Craig. I had been following the show, and he seemed like a nice enough fellow. However, when he announced that he was donating his winnings to a friend, a young woman called Joanne with Down's syndrome, so that she could go to America for a life-saving heart and lung transplant, he became my favourite person ever. Unfortunately though, this story does not have a happy ending either. Joanne turned out to be unsuitable for the surgery, and she died eight years later, aged 25. It broke my heart when I heard she could not be saved. After a while though, I tried to think about it differently; we all die, and many die too soon, but Joanne was really lucky to have been surrounded by so much love during the short time she was with her family and friends. That's the way I want to think about it.

Another positive media event came in 2016, when actress and comedian Sally Phillips (who has an adorable son called Olly, with Down's syndrome) created *A World Without Down's Syndrome?* for the BBC, possibly in response to the furore that Richard Dawkins had created with his comments. Sally's film was a sensitive and though-provoking documentary which explored the subject of pre-natal testing and termination. Sally made the case very well that the world is better place with Down's syndrome in it, and she is extremely positive about the condition. This film was so moving and so personal, that, even though I saw it several years after finishing writing this book, I felt I had to congratulate and thank her by adding a mention of it to this chapter, and by sending her a copy of the new edition. Hello Sally!

(By the way, Sally and I now follow each other on Twitter. If that makes me sound like I am bragging about my showbiz friends, let me just add that I know she only followed me back because I accidentally catfished her. I was running a spoof Peter Dinklage account at the time - I am a *Game of Thrones* fan, of course - and she thought I was him. Sorry Sally.)

Anyway, the point I am trying to make is that I have found, with a few exceptions like Sally's documentary and *The Last Leg*, that the way the media handles disability and Down's syndrome in particular, has been somewhat disappointing.

There is, however a place on the internet where you can go and feel good about Down's syndrome, and that place is the blogs. The internet is packed with loving parents blogging about their children with Down's syndrome, and they all seem so positive about it. So many of them say they are happy to have a child with special needs. The word "blessed" comes up a lot. For research purposes, I read a lot of these blogs. After a while, I started to think to myself how great this lifestyle sounded, and I actually caught myself feeling a little envious, and wishing I had a child with Down's syndrome. Then I remembered that I do.

Chapter 13: The Blogosphere

The worldwide web is full of blogs by parents of
children with Down's syndrome. There are millions
of them. Well...thousands of them. I did a quick
Google search and I found hundreds of them.
Well...dozens of them anyway. Here are just a few:

Not a Perfect Mom's Blog
Lila's Miracle Life
Starr Life
The Amazing Ella Grace
Unringing the Bell
Bringing The Sunshine
The Bates Motel
Noah's Dad
A Perfect Lily
The Future's Rosie
Trisomy Twenty-ONEderful
Those Newmans
Up The Down Staircase
What A Difference A Day Makes
Osoronut
Wee Pie And Little Sweetie
Our Dream Come True
4 Guys And A Lady
The Lucky Ten Percent

Living a Joyful Life with Down syndrome
All Are Precious in His Sight
The Blessing of Verity
Downs Side Up
Praying for Parker
Blessed By Leo
Wonderfully Made

They are all very different. Some look quite professional, others have just been put together quickly. Some are funny, some tell sad stories.

The one thing they all have in common though, is how much their owners love their children, and how much they enjoy being a parent of a child with Down's syndrome. I looked hard for a Down's syndrome blog written by a bitter and disillusioned parent, but could not find one. Of course it could be that there are thousands of such parents out there and they have all understandably chosen not to blog about their bitterness and disillusionment, but I am going to choose to ignore that possibility and focus on the positive blogs instead.

One of my favourite blogs is "The Amazing Ella Grace", written by Ella's mum, Kacey.

> My life was turned upside down when my daughter was born and surprised us all by having Down syndrome. Since her birth I

have come from sorrow and a sense of loss to greater happiness than I ever imagined and I owe it all to The Amazing Ella Grace!

Here is one typical post from Kacey:

Cayce (a little girl in Ella's class) brought Ella a necklace and a picture, and how sweet it was when she gave it to Ella.

The school bell rang and out came Ella. She ran up to me and excitedly showed me her necklace. It's a "Best Friend" necklace, the kind where one person has the "Best" half and the other has the "Friends" half. It was all I could do to not break down and cry right there at the front door of the school. Seriously melt my heart!!! I'm not sure how to say what this represents to me. I'm sure a lot of people will think it's silly that I am so excited about a necklace. But it's not just about the necklace. It's about my child having a real connection with another child. It's about another little girl thinking about my Ella outside of the classroom. It's about another parent allowing her child to have a friendship with a little girl with Down syndrome. It's about the pure love and excitement that shows on Ella's face when she wears her necklace and talks about her FRIEND Cayce!

I know it is the sort of story that makes internet trolls angry. I can visualise one now, sat under his bridge, typing furiously, "How DARE this Kacey person think anyone might want to hear about their child's life!" but for those of us who actually have souls, it is difficult not to be moved.

Here's another cute posting, this time from Tom, the author of "The Future's Rosie" and father of two year old Rosie (or "Bud", geddit?):

> Lately I've enjoyed sitting back and observing Bud, seeing how she chooses to amuse herself. She shuffles around the house finding things to play with and/or destroy. If she isn't playing or throwing something half way across the room she'll be sat there chatting to it. She's that sociable she will chat to anything, chair legs, the bin, her books...you name it! It's pretty safe to say however, that when her brothers are about not much else in the house gets a look in, least of all me! Just the other day the boys were playing out in the garden enjoying a rare spell of Northern sunshine and there was Rosie pressed up against the patio doors totally engrossed in her brothers. She sat there for ages laughing away to herself at all their silly antics!

And here is another from Michelle, the author of Big Blueberry Eyes. Michelle has some lovely photos on her blog (why don't mine come out like that?) and she also writes uplifting stories about her daughter Kayla:

> Earlier this summer we were walking back home from the end of our block. Kids were outside playing and Kayla stopped to play with a few girls who were jumping rope with a large rope. Each girl was on the other side of the street, the rope being long enough, and one taking turns jumping.
>
> I stayed on the sidewalk watching, and waiting, for Kayla. She took her turn holding the rope, but she's not as coordinated as the other girls. She tried to swing her arm in time with the girl on the other end. They were patient with her and attempted a few jumps when they could.
>
> I was standing by a vacant house when 3 cars pulled in to the driveway. I remember thinking to myself, "Wow someone is actually coming by to look at that house." The for sale sign had been in the yard for months.
>
> A few days later there was a moving truck in that driveway.

On one of our walks we met 2 of the 3 girls from the family. A week or so later I met their mom.

The mom told me that the day they were looking at the house she saw the girls playing outside. She said she watched them play for about 30 minutes. (She and the realtor were outside for several minutes waiting for her husband to arrive). She continued to tell me that she watched the girls with Kayla; she watched how they treated her, how they were with her, how they included her, how all the kids on the street were just out playing.

She said, "After watching them with your daughter I said, yep, this is the house, the street where I want to live."

Many bloggers tell the story of their child's birth, and the shock they felt when given the diagnosis. Here is Amy's story, from the blog "A Different View":

Ella was born 3 weeks early on Friday November 26th 2010 at 6.15pm after a relatively short and very straightforward labour. It never crossed either of our minds that anything was, or could be wrong. She struggled to breastfeed after her birth, and I was given help overnight to cup feed her by a student midwife. Looking back, during that night I must have seen every member of staff that was on duty. They came in by 'accident', to fetch equipment or because I had pressed the call bell. Despite their differing reasons for being in the room, they all came and looked at Ella. This didn't strike me as odd at the time, but with hindsight, I now understand why.

The next day, we received the news that Ella was displaying several features of a baby with Down's syndrome. Shock and devastation set in and a million and one questions immediately started racing through our heads. This wasn't at all what we had expected. Instead of taking our beautiful girl home, we were having to readjust our hopes and dreams and face up to a future of uncertainty.

Looking back at that night, I did have my suspicions. It makes me smile now, as I remember checking her palm creases - one of the features of Down's syndrome is a singular palmar crease. Ella has normal palmar creases but she does have the wide set, almond shaped eyes and small nose that characterise facial features of people with Down's syndrome.

Once we were told, we had little time to react to the news as Ella dropped her blood sugar, temperature and oxygen saturations and was taken to Neonatal Intensive Care

> Unit (NICU). It was thought that she had a heart defect, which up to 50% of babies born with Down's syndrome do.

> A heart scan the next morning showed she did have a hole in the wall of her heart. We were told this was manageable with medication but that she would need surgery when she was 4-6 months old.

Amy, however, like all the other bloggers I read, goes on to say that once the initial shock wore off, things seemed so much better:

> If you had told me then that I would feel as happy and as blessed as I do today, I wouldn't have believed you. Not for a second.

Rick, the author of "Noah's Dad", holds the same view:

> If I could go back in time and just tell myself one thing when I first learned Noah had Down syndrome it would be:

> Rick, things are going to be just fine, trust me. This next year is going to be the best year of your life. I know it doesn't feel that way now, but trust me on this one!

> And today, one year later, on my son's first birthday, I can confirm 100% that the above statement is true. This year truly has been

the best year of my life. There are no words
to describe how much I love my son and
how much joy he brings to our life.

This is a fine sentiment, and one I share myself. I
would love to be able to go back in time and reassure
the younger me; however, I think if I could only tell
myself one thing at the beginning of the last decade, it
would be to buy shares in Apple and Google.

Patti is the author of "A Perfect Lily". She is also a
great photographer (perhaps there is something
wrong with my camera), and mother of eleven
children (at the time of going to press), including Lily,
who has Down's syndrome. Patti writes
enthusiastically:

FACT: Babies with Down syndrome are so
stinking cute you just might pass out from
cuteness overload.

FACT: Babies with Down syndrome are so
irresistible that you might never be able to
take your eyes off them.

FACT: Down syndrome produces an
overabundance of the "adorable" gene.

FACT: Once you have a child with Down
syndrome you will find yourself addicted to
almond eyed smiles, crooked pinkies, and
sandal gap toes. There is no known cure.

> FACT: Down syndrome produces
> irreversible enlargement of the heart. Once
> you experience life with an extra
> chromosome, you will have more
> compassion, love, and appreciation for life
> than you know what to do with.

Hayley Goleniowska is a campaigner, aiming to change perceptions of Down's syndrome through her blog "Downs Side Up".

> Natalia was born at home, silent and blue,
> the dash to the Neonatal Intensive Care unit
> revealing a diagnosis of Down's syndrome,
> along with two small holes in her heart. The
> words punched through my soul. The
> bottom of my world dropped from beneath
> me and dark fear, worry and shock rushed
> in; I hadn't signed up for this! Why me? But
> seven years on, having walked the path I
> was so adamant that I didn't want to take, I
> now know 'why me'. I cannot re-live those
> early days with the knowledge I now have,
> but I can enlighten other parents.

She tackles serious subjects like "The Sugar-Coated Disability Abortion Lie", and "Outshining the Bigots", but she is also pretty down-to-earth, and not above posting stories like "Poogate", the tale of the badly-timed poo in a posh car showroom:

"I'm sorry but I need to get some things out of the boot of my car. There's been a bottom explosion."

Silence and a polite smile.

"Er...my daughter not me, ha!" (nervous smile).

"Of course."

Then the smile of a man who was clearly a father, and probably a very good one, although I sensed his days of embarrassing poo incidents were way behind him. Perhaps he remembered them with a certain amount of nostalgia? Will I ever look back at these incidents with fondness?

There are also a lot of blogs by parents of children with autism – a quick Google search brings out the most popular ones "Love, Belief and Balls", "Flappiness Is…", "Squidalicious", "We go with him", the list goes on and on.

Because of the nature of autism though, the children these blogs refer to are all very very different. Some children are high functioning, others are low functioning, even non-verbal. The parents can have very different views on autism. There is a spectrum.

"Autism Daddy" says:

> I LOVE my son, but I don't love his autism. He was given a raw deal. He has severe autism and it gets in his way with EVERYTHING. So this page will be 75% comically ranting & complaining & telling it like it is and 25% inspirational & warm & cuddly & feel good stories...

Novelist Kathy Lette however, has this to say about her high-functioning grown-up son, who has Asperger's syndrome:

> Yes, my life with Julius is challenging, but it's also hilarious, humbling, and enriching. My kind, clever, quirky boy has now grown into a handsome young man who is the most interesting and courageous person I have ever met.

For both autism and Down's syndrome, navigating the Blogosphere is a tricky thing. Finding the right blog that speaks to you out of the thousands that are out there is not easy, but I hope that I have given you a starting point if you decide you want to give it a go.

Blogs were not around when Jamie was born. If they had been then maybe they would have helped me and Meg, by telling us what to expect, and making the whole thing less scary for us. I am sure they are a great help to the parents of children newly diagnosed with Down's syndrome and/or ASD.

However, if I am honest, despite the occasional stories about poo, none of the children in these blogs really remind me of Jamie.

What I really wanted to read was a blog about a child with Down's syndrome, autism, and ADHD, which told funny stories about the mischief he got up to. I could not find one, so I wrote my own.

Chapter 14: Traffic Light

When Jamie was aged 11, I started to keep a blog.

I thought it might be therapeutic for me, and it was. I really did enjoy the writing process. Unfortunately, not knowing anything about internet marketing, I failed to attract any "traffic" (that means "readers", in internet parlance, it has nothing to do with vehicular transport). At its peak, the blog was getting up to three readers per day. That was only on a good day though.

For that reason, I feel safe reproducing some of my favourite blog posts here, confident that you won't have read them before.

February 12th - The Prisoner

"If ever you are going to be trapped in a tiny room for hours on end, the downstairs toilet would be the best room for it to happen in. Unlike, say, a lift, a sauna, or a cupboard, our downstairs toilet has running water, somewhere to sit down, and most importantly, it has a toilet. It also has a small window that you could open for fresh air, or possibly even call for help from - or at least it would have had such a thing if we had not locked it in order to stop Jamie from throwing the toilet rolls out of it."

This, she told me later, was what Meg was thinking when, as you have probably guessed, Jamie trapped her in the downstairs toilet. She had popped in for a few seconds to powder her nose, when the door closed behind her, and she heard a loud crash from outside. Jamie had pulled the radiator off the wall, and it had fallen in front of the toilet door.

I imagine that many of you reading this have never seen a radiator that has been pulled from a wall. I had not, until recently. I would have thought that the act of pulling it from the wall would also have broken the pipes attached to it, leading to water gushing everywhere and a massive plumber's bill, but no. Somehow, the pipes at the bottom of the radiator remained intact, and the whole thing swivelled away from the wall and landed in front of the toilet door. Being a heavy radiator, and still being attached to the wall via the pipes, it would not move at all, and the door could not be opened more than a centimetre or two. Perhaps it would have been possible to force the door open, but that would certainly have broken the pipes, and probably the door too.

So Meg was trapped.

Jamie, on the other hand, now had the run of the house. He finally had the freedom to do whatever he wanted. He could eat all the chocolate in the sweet drawer, shred every piece of paper in the office, microwave the guinea pigs ... or he could just hunt around for where Meg had hidden the house keys, unlock the door, and go exploring around the neighbourhood.

How long would Meg be trapped for? Well, I work in an office 30 minutes' drive away, so if she could have called me at work, I could have been home in half an hour. However, her mobile phone was on the kitchen windowsill, not in her pocket. My working day was 9am to 5pm. Unfortunately it was only 10:15am, so it was over 7 hours before I would be due to return.

Fortunately though, it was actually a Saturday, and I was not at work at all - I was upstairs, wondering what the crash was. When I heard "Steve! I'm trapped in the toilet!" shouted a few seconds later, I thought I had better go and investigate.

April 27th - Crack Problem

We had forgotten to give Jamie a travel sickness pill. Normally, we can drive at least 45 minutes without any risk of car sickness, and sometimes an hour. This journey, according to the Satnav, was 52 minutes. Trying to drive all that way without stopping would be a gamble.

We were twenty minutes into the journey when Meg said "Open Jamie's window just a tiny bit, and give him some fresh air."

Doing this would also be a risk. We both knew that Jamie likes nothing better than livening up a boring car journey by throwing things out of the window - his shoes, his socks, my sunglasses, the Satnav - whatever he can reach really. This is why we always have the car windows shut and the child locks on.

"Just a tiny bit then," I said. "Hold his hands while I do it - if I open it too far, you know what will happen."

So Meg held his hands, and I lightly flicked the relevant button. I need not have worried about opening it too far. I judged it right first time, and the window opened by about a centimetre. Meg released Jamie's hands, and relaxed. There was no way that anything he could reach was going to fit through that tiny crack.

Or so we thought. Jamie sat and studied the situation for a while. He made no attempt to grab anything and force it through, but he scanned round the car with his eyes, mentally calculating whether anything was going to fit. In an attempt to stay one step ahead, Meg moved everything that was less than five centimetres thick to the other side of the vehicle.

So we continued on our journey for about another minute or two. All of a sudden I heard Meg shouting behind me.

"No Jamie! Stop that! Aaaargh! You naughty boy! That was brand new!"

Startled, I looked in the rear view mirror. I saw Jamie looking back at me, trying to look as though nothing out of the ordinary had happened. There was something different about him. Wasn't he wearing a baseball cap a few minutes ago?

Yes, even though a baseball cap appears to be as big as your head, the truth is that you can feed the peak of the cap through a very small opening, as Jamie had instinctively known you could, and had proved. I would have thought that main body of the cap would have got stuck, but no, it did not. Perhaps the wind took it and sucked it through. It was all over in a second.

"Sorry," said Jamie. But I don't think he was.

I got the hat back eventually. We were on a busy A road, and I had to drive on a few hundred yards before finding somewhere I could stop the car, then run back down the road. There was no footpath, so I was dodging speeding cars and lorries, to rescue the cap that was sat in the middle of the road, on a white line. It was good exercise for me, and the way I see it, the fact that I could have been run over and killed, just gave me the opportunity to appreciate life more.

That's not really true, I just like to end on a positive note.

Oh, and one other positive note - the unscheduled stop broke up the journey, and Jamie did not get travel sickness after all. Hmmm ... I wonder if that was his plan all along?

May 10th – Vintage Pornography

I have a new smart phone.

It looks great and works perfectly. I mention this because I want to remember the feeling. I know it won't last for long, because soon, Jamie will break it. Perhaps he will knock it out of my hand, and it will fall on the floor and shatter, like the last one? Or perhaps I will leave it lying around and he will throw it out of a first floor window, like the one before that?

I am just savouring the moment - enjoying being at the forefront of technology (well, within sight of the forefront) for once. I know that before long my lovely phone will be destroyed, and I will have to go back to using that little blue phone with the scratched screen that I bought in 2002 that Jamie, for some reason, never feels the urge to destroy.

While feeding Jamie yesterday, I noticed that my new phone has a voice recognition feature that allows you to use Google to search the internet by speaking into it rather than typing. I decided to test it out, and thought for a second about what I would like to search for.

I have an interest in classic films (I actually run a moderately successful website on the subject) so, speaking loudly and clearly, I said into my phone "Black and white movies".

Jamie, who was sat next to me, objected to this for some reason, and shouted out "No daddy!" My phone heard what he said, and tagged his words onto the end of the search. Unfortunately though, because his diction is not great, it misheard him. I looked at my phone and found that instead of Googling "black and white movies no daddy" I had Googled "black and white movies nudity".

What worries me about this is that I know Google records all these search terms, and has an algorithm to work out what sort of interests people have. So I am probably now on a list somewhere of people who are sexually interested in people from the 1940s. If old age pensioners start disappearing in my area I am going to get a knock on the door.

I am just glad I did not say "children's movies".

May 28th – The Disability Living Allowance Form has Killed my Soul

Right, it's that time again. I have to fill in the form to renew my disability living allowance. Interestingly, I know that I filled the form in a few years ago, but I really cannot remember a thing about it. It is as though I have wiped it from my mind for some reason. Why would I do that?

Ah well, not to worry. I'll make a start now, it should only take ten minutes or so. Gosh, it's a big booklet though isn't it? Maybe half an hour...

Name of child:

No problem there. If all the questions are like this then this is going to be a doddle

Child reference number:

Ha ha! Also no problem - that was on the letter they sent with the form.

Date of birth, sex, address, nationality,...

This is going to be easy

In the last 12 months, has the child seen anyone apart from their GP about their illnesses or disabilities?

He has seen loads of doctors, psychiatrists, social workers, therapists, not to mention the experts they have at his special-needs school. If I tick the "yes" box though I am going to have to find out all their names, addresses, phone numbers and area of speciality. Bugger. How am I going to do that? I just took him along to all the appointments they arranged for him. I did not take minutes. Maybe his mother will know? I will come back to this question.

Do you have any reports, letters or assessments about the child's illnesses or disabilities?

I think there was something about a year ago. Now where did I put it? Oh dear, I am starting to get a sinking feeling about this. How many questions are there on this form?...[flicking to back of booklet] ... Sixty four!!! Holy crap, this is going to take all weekend.

Statement from someone who knows the child:

Well I know him, can I do it? I suspect not but it doesn't say explicitly either way on the form. I guess

156

I am going to have to look in the information booklet
... [checks booklet]...well that was no use at all. Sigh. I
suppose I could get one of his teachers to make a
statement next week.

List the child's illnesses or disabilities:

I was wondering when they were going to ask that.
He's got Down's syndrome and autism and ADHD,
just like he had the last time I filled in this form a few
years ago. Is there a box I can tick that says nothing
has changed since the last time I applied? No, of
course not.

How long has he had the disabilities?

Since birth. Well actually, since before birth - I
believe something went wrong in one of the very first
cell divisions. How accurate do I need to be? Am I
going to need to look it up on Wikipedia?

What treatment does he have for it?

Treatment? What does that mean? Does special
school count?

How often does he have treatment?

Er...

Can he physically walk?

Oh yes, he can walk. However, he prefers to RUN. Yes, he runs like a gazelle evading a pack of hungry lions. You just take your eye off him for a second and he is off. Where to? It doesn't matter - towards busy traffic, open water, a sheer drop - he doesn't care, it's fun.

How far can he walk?

I will tick the highest box - over 200m. (I assume that is metres, not miles.)

How long does it take him?

"How long" is not really the point. Walking really isn't a big problem, as I have mentioned.

What is his walking speed?

There isn't a box labelled "gazelle".

Does he need encouragement or help to go to the toilet?

Oh this is depressing. I am going to have to tell them
I am still wiping for him. At least he has stopped
smearing poo on the walls now.

Does he have any hobbies?

Does smashing toys count as a hobby?

*Lots and lots of questions about bedtime, mealtimes, dressing,
eyesight, communication...*

Oh I have had enough of this. He's got Down's
syndrome with severe behavioural problems - surely
the people reading the form know what that means.

I really cannot face this anymore. I can feel my soul
dying inside me. I no longer fear death as much as I
did an hour ago [Throws pen across room].

Let's just not claim shall we? We don't really need the
money; we aren't poor. How much money is it
anyway? How much? Really? Oh.

Did anyone see where that pen went?

If you live in Wales and would like us to contact you in Welsh, tick this box:

Don't tempt me.

June 4th – Heeere's Jamie

Jamie used to kick holes in his bedroom wall. We are not sure why. At one point, a few months ago, there were holes in the wall, pieces of plaster everywhere, the bed was broken, the curtain rail and curtains were in a pile in the corner of the room, and there was so much mess on the floor that you could not see the carpet. It was like a crack den.

So, we got a man in. A real man that is, one who can do handyman stuff, unlike me (my father-in-law as it happens), and had the walls reinforced with wood panelling.

Since we had the walls reinforced, Jamie can no longer kick holes in them, and so he kicked a hole in his bedroom door instead. It took him ages to do it; you have to admire his dedication - it was like a cross between *The Shawshank Redemption* and *The Shining*.

I think he regrets it now, because it means we can spy on him in his bedroom, from the corridor. The other day we were sat outside watching him play with his Toy Story figures. Jessie was in a lot of trouble, which involved screaming, then Buzz and Woody rescued her, I think…or possibly murdered her - it's impossible to be certain. Anyway, the point is we are normally forced to leave the room when he is playing, but now he cannot stop us watching.

So, I don't mind the hole too much. It looks a bit untidy though; perhaps we should put a window in. Or a cat-flap! A cat-flap would be cool.

One thing does worry me, and that is the fact that the inside of the door seems to be made from cardboard.

July 14th – Chocolate Surprise

Meg has just run past me in the hallway carrying a small bowl of soapy water, and a cloth. I asked her what was wrong and she said "Jamie has rubbed chocolate into the carpet." As she climbed the stairs though, she added ruefully "...at least, I hope it's chocolate."

I thought for a second, then shouted after her up the stairs "If ever I write a book, that's what I am going to call it – *At Least I Hope it's Chocolate*."

[I changed my mind. In the end it did not even become a chapter heading]

Chapter 15: Down by Law

I opened the front door to find two police officers stood on the doorstep. One was black, the other white, both were male and in their thirties, powerfully built, and with stern expressions on their faces.

"Good evening sir." said one. "We are responding to an emergency call that was placed from this address a short while ago."

"Er … no, I think… I mean, there's no … erm … "

I think I might have panicked a little; I am not used to being interrogated by the police. I remember one time I met a fellow parent who introduced himself to me as a policeman; all he did was ask me what I did for a living, and within seconds I found myself confessing that when I was seventeen I got drunk and fell asleep in a bus shelter and got told to move by a local bobby.

I have watched a lot of crime drama over the years, and I understand the importance of being cool and not incriminating yourself, but the reality of being questioned by the police is quite different from TV and movies. As these two policemen stood in my doorway, I knew that I had not committed a crime, and the pressure these two officers were putting me under was nothing like I had seen in *Prime Suspect*, but I was falling apart anyway. They were not going to need *Cracker* to break me down.

Luckily, Meg turned up to rescue me.

"What's the problem?"

"Madam, an emergency call was placed from the address a short while ago, and the caller was in distress."

Meg thought for a second, then laughed nervously. "Oh, that will be my son. He has Down's syndrome. And he's autistic. He sometimes picks up the phone and presses random buttons. He shouts a lot too."

While Meg was talking to one of the officers, the other was glaring at me. I started to feel uncomfortable as I realised that the officer was suspicious. I guess that police officers get to see a lot of domestic violence. This one clearly thought that I had been beating someone, possibly Meg, or maybe Jamie, and that now Meg and I were both trying to cover it up.

I looked him in the eye and said "Screw you, copper! You ain't got nuffink on me!" I did not say it out loud, obviously, that would have been stupid.

Meg was, you will be relieved to hear, telling the truth. Jamie does indeed like to press random buttons on the phone if you leave him alone with it for more than thirty seconds. He has discovered that most of the time, pressing buttons makes a human voice come onto the other end. Usually, the voice says "The number you have dialled has not been recognised. Please hang up and try again." From Jamie's point of view, this is fine as far as it goes. However, when he dialled 999 that evening, and found a person on the other end who said something different, and who was actually prepared to have a conversation with him, he must have thought it was his birthday. Sadly for us though, Jamie's conversation technique sounded to the 999 operator like somebody being assaulted.

I have never beaten anybody in my family. I don't expect credit for that. Hopefully, saying that "I have never beaten anybody in my family" should elicit the same response from you as if I had said "I have never mugged a blind woman" or "I have never put a cat in a wheelie bin." That is, I would expect you to shrug, and say, "Of course, that goes without saying."

Meg and I have had a lot to deal with, and we have both been under a lot of pressure at various points over the years. I have heard that a lot of marriages collapse under the sort of pressure that we have experienced. Many marriages don't survive the stress of having a disabled child, and I sympathise with those people. However, for me and Meg, the difficulties just brought us closer together. From the very beginning we both knew that raising Jamie would be a challenge that we would face together. We were partners in every sense of the word. We were not going to let each other down.

The reason I feel the need to explicitly deny any wrongdoing, is that I am convinced some people think that I am guilty. The thing is, Meg bruises very easily. This fact, combined with the fact that she is naturally very clumsy, has often led to her going into work with visible bruises. The worst time was a year or so before we were married, and she crashed her car. She was not badly hurt but she did have two black eyes that lasted for a fortnight. I could feel strangers glaring accusingly at me whenever we went out anywhere together, but nobody ever said anything.

Over the years she has fallen down the stairs, and up the stairs, and if there is a slippery surface somewhere in the house, she will find it and slip on it. One time quite recently, Meg did literally walk into a door, and broke a rib. She made up a different story for her work colleagues though, because "I walked into a door" is a well-known euphemism for "My husband beats me but I don't want to talk about it." Even as I write this, she has a big purple and yellow bruise on her shoulder shaped like a map of Texas, which she somehow acquired on the dodgem cars at a funfair in Northumberland.

Jamie doesn't help the situation either. He does like a bit of rough and tumble, and he doesn't always know his own strength. This often results in bruises for Meg too. Somebody at work once took her aside to ask her about bruises on her arms that were clearly hand prints. It was Jamie's hand.

I get bruises too of course. In fact, on the occasion that the police knocked on my door, I did actually have a big bruise on my knee at the time. A few days earlier I had fallen over while chasing Jamie through the Oxford Natural History Museum, trying to catch him before he reached the inadequately fenced-off display of dinosaur skeletons. The bruise was on my knee though, and it never seemed like the right moment in the conversation to roll up my trouser leg and say "What do you think of that officer?"

The two police officers seemed reluctant to accept our explanation that the phone call had been made by a child with special needs. One of them asked Meg if he could come in, and would she like to talk to him alone? Meg repeated the story about Jamie's habit of making random phone calls, still trying to laugh it off, but she was starting to get a little flustered, and even I started to think she was acting guilty.

She told me later that the reason she got flustered was she had suddenly become very aware of the fact that she was wearing her pyjamas. She was feeling self-conscious, not making eye-contact, and generally wanting the conversation to finish as soon as possible. Unfortunately for us though, the police officers had seen her discomfort and assumed that there was something sinister going on.

Our story was not helped by the fact that Jamie was nowhere to be seen. In the eleven years that I had known him, this was the first time ever that the doorbell had rung and he had not come to investigate who it was. There had been many an occasion where I had been unable to get rid of people on my doorstep who were trying to persuade me to join their religion, or perhaps their gas and electricity supplier, because Jamie had turned up and tried to engage them in conversation (by which I mean he stared at them until it became awkward for all of us). Not on this occasion though. I could hear him in his bedroom listening to a CD of *The Ting Tings*. Eventually, I decided to go and fetch him. As soon as the police officers saw him I knew they would be convinced. I ran upstairs and into his bedroom, and said "Come and see who is at the door Jamie!"

At this point, the story I am telling you could have gone one of two ways. The first way is that Jamie could have co-operated fully and come downstairs to see the policemen, who would then have realized that no crime had been committed, and been on their way. The second way is that he could have refused to come downstairs, and started yelling and throwing things about the bedroom until one of the policemen came bounding up the stairs, burst through the door, and taught me the meaning of the phrase "police brutality". Can you guess which way it went?

It was the first way.

You probably think that that is a good thing, from my point of view. Of course, at the time, I was relieved. Looking back now though, as I sit at this computer writing this so-called "comedy memoir", I am a little frustrated, because it would have made a much better story if it had gone the second way. I suspect that Jamie planned this whole thing from beginning to end, including the fact that the story would not have a resolution that was satisfying enough to use as an anecdote.

I could have lied of course, and told you that the story went the second way. I could probably have justified it in my head as not really being a lie, merely an embellishment. But I want this book to be as true as possible.

And that brings us to my final story about Jamie. It is a story that I have not been looking forward to telling you, but there is no putting it off any longer. I have just spent the last chapter convincing you that I have never deliberately hurt anybody in my family, and that is true, but there was a time I hurt somebody without meaning to. It was an accident.

Chapter 16: The Accident

It was a Saturday morning, and like most Saturday mornings, I had taken Jamie for a trip out, to give Meg a break. I thought it was important that Meg had the opportunity to rest whenever possible, but also it was something that I enjoyed doing – I enjoyed spending time with him, having fun with him. Usually we would go to a park, or a castle or stately home with nice grounds, somewhere Jamie could run around. He loved to run around.

On this occasion I had taken him to Gloucester. A travelling fair was in town, and I was sure he would love it. Jamie usually enjoyed the rides, the bright lights, and the noise, but for some reason this time he did not seem in the mood - he was very quiet, and said he wanted to go home shortly after we arrived. I took him back to the car and he was clearly not himself. He was becoming more and more subdued. As I was putting his seat belt on for him, he did not even try to lick my cheek. Something was obviously wrong.

On the journey home I kept a close eye on him in the rear view mirror. Whenever Jamie is in the car with me, I am always on high alert for signs of travel sickness. I have promised myself that I won't get caught out again like the time I did driving through the Cotswolds a few years ago, when I ignored the signs of sickness, trying to make it home before Jamie was ill, only to have him projectile vomit all the way from the back seat to the windscreen at the front. On that occasion my head was protected from the worst of it by the headrest on the seat, but I will never forget the feeling I had seeing the noxious spray in my peripheral vision go past me on both sides.

Seeing that Jamie seemed to be getting worse, and keen to avoid a repetition of the Cotswolds incident, I asked him if he was feeling sick, and he said yes. I pulled over and got out the plastic bowl that I now always keep in the car. A few seconds later, he threw up.

I was puzzled. It was true that Jamie did often suffer from travel sickness, but normally that did not take hold until after about an hour's driving, and we had only been going for about ten minutes. I could not blame the fairground rides either – he had only been on a couple of them, and they were not what you would call intense rides (unless you have a phobia of miniature fire engines going slowly round in a circle).

I comforted Jamie, and after a while, when he told me (unconvincingly) that he was feeling better, we resumed our journey. As we were driving along I began to think about what could be causing the illness, and something started to nag at me from the corner of my mind. Just before leaving the house that morning I had given him some medication; it was a drug that he had been taking for several weeks to help manage his behaviour. One of Jamie's specialists had been trying to persuade us for some time to try him on a certain drug, and we had finally agreed, thinking that if it affected him aversely we could always just stop.

The medication was a syrupy liquid. It did not taste too bad, but even so, Jamie would never take it, so we always mixed it into his breakfast yogurt. The thing that was worrying me was, how much of the drug had I given him that morning? Giving him the medicine had become part of the daily routine over the past few weeks, and as a result of this I often did it on autopilot, without really thinking about it, and then forgot about it straight away. However, I was starting to remember that that morning had been a little different. I had not been able to find the little plastic syringe that we used to measure out the dosage. I had known though, that the dosage was the same as a teaspoon, because I could visualise drawing the fluid up to the "5" mark, and a teaspoon is 5ml. So that is what I had given him - a teaspoon-full. Now however, I was starting to have doubts - did it say 5 on the syringe ... or did it say 0.5? I suddenly had a sickening feeling - had I got it wrong? Had I given Jamie a massive overdose?

Grimly, I put my foot down on the accelerator, and got both of us home as quickly as I could. Jamie was looking much worse and I had to carry him into the house and lay him down on the sofa. I muttered something to Meg who was understandably looking alarmed, then I ran upstairs to the bathroom cabinet. I tugged the door open and grabbed the little brown bottle that was at the front. My eyes scanned the label looking for the dosage information. I found it - children under 12... 0.5ml. My heart sank. I had given him ten times too much.

A feeling of dread gripped me as I realised I was going to have to go and tell Meg that I had poisoned our son. I did not want to do it; I wanted to lock the bathroom door and lie on the floor. I knew though, that every second I delayed was putting Jamie at risk, so I did not hesitate for more than an instant. I forced my legs to carry me back downstairs and into the living room. I had no idea how best to break the bad news, so I just said it.

"I gave Jamie too much medicine this morning."

"How much too much?"

"Ten times."

I shut my eyes and waited for the howl of anguish, or perhaps the torrent of anger that would come my way; but Meg took it calmly. She told me to call 999, which I did, then she went back to tending to her son, who was motionless on the sofa, and starting to look a little green. I stood back, watching helplessly, as Meg's nursing training and experience came through. She cleaned him, made him comfortable, and made sure he was not scared.

I was scared though. What the hell had I done? After all those years of looking after him, learning new skills every day to protecting him from the most unexpected and unlikely dangers, I had failed Jamie with my inability to tell the difference between 5 and 0.5 – me, a professional mathematician, brought down by a misplaced decimal point.

I expected Meg to be furious with me. I was thinking about how cross she had been with me when I had forgotten to buy milk on my way home from work the day before. That was a silly mistake; this was the worst thing I had ever done. She was not furious though – she could see how upset I was, how close I was to collapsing into a heap. She just took my hand, and squeezed it gently.

After the longest fifteen minutes of our lives, an ambulance pulled up outside the house, and two paramedics, both women, got out and started walking towards the front door. I opened it before they had had a chance to knock, and started to explain the situation straight away. Within seconds one of them was examining Jamie, and the other was examining the medication bottle.

The pair of them discussed Jamie's symptoms, and the active ingredients in the medication. Meg listened intently, but the language they used did not mean very much to me.

One of them then produced a mobile phone and made a call to what I presume was some sort of poison control hotline, because she was reading out the active ingredients of the medication to the person on the other end of the line. After a while she stopped talking, and started listening, occasionally interjecting a "Hmmm", "Oh", or "I see."

Eventually the conversation finished and she hung up. She put the phone back into her pocket, and turned to me with a worried look in her eye. She said that they were going to have to take Jamie to hospital.

I nodded. Still, at this point, I found myself unable to ask the question that I most desperately needed to know the answer to – the question I had wanted to ask since the moment the paramedics had arrived, but had been too afraid to.

Was he going to die?

Chapter 17: Jemima

When we found out that Meg was pregnant again, we were both thrilled. A small piece of me did feel guilty though - it felt as though we were replacing Jamie.

I felt guilty because I knew that this new baby did not have Down's syndrome (we had had the pre-natal test done), and I knew that she (the test had also told us it was a baby girl) would be the baby I had always wanted. I knew that one day I would be helping her with schoolwork, offering advice on relationships, teaching her to drive, and generally doing all the normal things that normal parenting involved. For some reason that I found difficult to understand, it felt like I was betraying the memory of Jamie's childhood. I had loved Jamie hadn't I? With all my heart? So why was it that I felt so excited that this new baby did not have Down's syndrome?

Most parents say that their second pregnancy is a lot more relaxed than the first one. I guess that might be true for parents who had not been through what we had been through. Even after we were told that the baby was healthy and normal, every doctor's appointment and every scan filled us with anxiety.

We were convinced that sooner or later, somebody was going to discover something terrible.

But they did not.

She was born a healthy 7 pounds and 13 ounces (not a massive 13 pounds and 7 ounces as I told everyone at work by email, for some reason), and she was perfect.

The fact that the baby was a girl did help with my guilt. It would have been okay, I think you will agree, for a parent who had had, say, five baby boys, to be especially thrilled to find out that the sixth baby was a girl; and in many ways, raising Jamie had been similar to raising five boys. Maybe six.

For the first couple of days she did not have a name, so Meg and I batted ideas around. Meg liked "Tabitha", but I thought it sounded a bit *too* middle class. It would be fine in Waitrose, but I knew that at some point in her life I would have to take her to McDonalds and ask her "What would you like to drink with your Big Mac, Tabitha?" and it just did not sound right.

We both liked "Verity" but then we realised that her initials would be VD.

We also considered Amelia, Maggie, Madeline, Isabel, Scarlett, Lucy, Rowena, Matilda, Olivia, Imogen,

Marianne, Holly, Lesley, Anne (after grandmothers, those last two) - but nothing seemed right.

Once or twice though, while holding my new daughter in my arms, I accidentally referred to her as "Jamie". Years of practice of holding a helpless infant called Jamie in my arms had conditioned me to think that was what they were all called. After a while, the name Jamie seemed to suit her.

"We need a name that is a bit like Jamie, but not Jamie." I said.

"How about Jemima?" said Meg. "That was on my list of suggestions that we talked about before she was born. You said you did not like it because it reminded you of the doll on Play School."

"I never said that!"

I had said it. But now, I had changed my mind.

"Jemima" it was.

Before long, the guilt passed. I just really loved being a dad to this beautiful little girl. Have I mentioned she was beautiful? I know that all fathers think that their daughters are beautiful, but let's be honest, some of them are just kidding themselves. Jemima really was beautiful though.

Raising Jemima has been as exciting and fulfilling as I could have hoped it would be. Meg and I finally got to be the sort of parents that other parents could speak to without any awkwardness. We finally got to go to see Italy after all.

Meg gave up her job completely for a while and became a full time mother, and she took the responsibility seriously, applying the same level of dedication as she had with Jamie when he was a baby.

We got to teach her to read, swim, and ride a bike (harder than I thought it was going to be, that one).

As she got older we watched movies together and talked about them afterwards, rather than having to leave half way through because somebody was throwing their shoes around the auditorium.

We could take her to museums and tell her about the exhibits, rather than just tell her not to chew the exhibits.

We helped her to make sense of the world.

Having had Jamie, and having gone through all the difficulties we had, really affected the sort of parents we were with Jemima. We appreciated the joys of parenthood (that phrase is often used sarcastically, but I really mean it) more than anyone else we knew. Jemima is at school now; we go to all her school plays and concerts, we make classroom visits, we go on school trips to help out, we cheer the loudest at sports days, we take her to fun and interesting places, we have her friends over for sleepovers, and we have the best birthday parties we can.

And we still don't have to go to football matches in the rain. Yeah!

And now Jem is reaching the age where I can really start to help her with her schoolwork. Some of her subjects are starting to get a little tricky, so I can become that great teacher that I always wanted to be. I said earlier that my dream, before Jamie was born, was that my son or daughter might surpass my own academic achievement. My view on this has changed now. I will always be there to help her, and Jemima is bright, so maybe she will do it, but really, it is not so important to me anymore.

I used to think that intelligence and academic excellence were the most important things that a child could achieve, but after all those years with Jamie, I realised that love is more important. I am acutely aware that I sound like a Hallmark card or the end of a black and white Christmas movie when I say that, and if I am honest I am not quite sure exactly what it means, but I am saying it anyway. I hope you forgive me being a little bit sentimental, as it is nearly the end of the book.

Where was I?

Oh yes, love.

We love Jemima. Jemima loves her mum and dad, and we all love her brother too.

Yes, that's right. We love her brother, Jamie, very much. Jamie is fine by the way. I am sorry if you thought for a few minutes, after the sudden end of the previous chapter, that something terrible had happened to him, but I did say at the beginning of the book that it was not going to be a misery memoir. I think I might even have underlined it. So it is your own fault really for not paying attention earlier.

No, Jamie is just fine. After the accidental overdose, the ambulance took him to the hospital for observation, and within a few hours it was clear from the observation that he was going to make a full recovery. Then a few hours after that, the observers observed him running around the ward pressing all the buttons he could find - flicking lights on and off, raising beds, turning off important medical equipment, and summoning nurses. When he started knocking drinks out of the hands of the other patients, the doctors decided that perhaps he did not have to stay overnight after all, and he was discharged.

In case you were wondering, all the hospital staff were really nice to me too, despite the whole thing being my stupid fault. Five different doctors told me what an easy mistake it was to make, and that *even doctors* did that sort of thing occasionally. I thanked them all, and decided not to tell them that I was a professional mathematician and that they could stick their patronizing attitudes up their arses. I decided against it because they were just being nice, and I was the idiot who had poisoned his son because he had been in too much of a hurry to read the instructions on the medicine bottle properly.

Instead, I took Jamie home, and we just got on with being a family. The four of us.

I feel I should mention that this incident took place several years after Jemima was born. I am afraid the chronology in this chapter is all over the place, and I apologize if it has left you scratching your head. When I planned it I was thinking it would be like a Tarantino movie, but if you wanted to call it "a confusing mess", I don't think I could really argue. It is at times like these that I wish I had a proper editor.

Jamie was four when Jemima was born. Let us just revisit that for a short while.

Being the parents of those two beautiful young children was the most amazing thing that ever happened to me and Meg, but it was bloody hard work, especially for Meg. We got to discover that normal parenting is not the walk in the park we had always assumed it would be. Okay, to be fair, there was a lot of walking in the park in the early days, but there were also a lot of difficulties too. The first year in particular was especially hard, as we had to cope with a baby and an extremely badly behaved little boy at the same time, on almost no sleep. (Yes, again. We had another non-sleeper. What are the odds?)

Jamie loved his baby sister; you could see it in the way he looked at her, and the way he held her so carefully. He would never have deliberately hurt Jem, but we could not be sure that he actually understood that he could hurt her without meaning to. It was a nervous time. For years I was convinced that his love of slamming doors was going to result in an accident that would curtail his sister's career as a concert pianist before it had even started. I also worried that he might hug her too hard, poke her in the eye, push her down the stairs, or throw something heavy at her. There was a minor scare once, when Jem was learning to crawl, and Jamie misread this as in invitation to ride her like a pony. No harm was done though. We were always vigilant, and nothing terrible ever actually happened. In the end, the thing that curtailed Jem's musical career was her complete lack of interest in learning to play the piano.

As she got older there were new difficulties. Alongside all the usual perils like road safety, stranger danger, school gate politics, and bullying, we had something else to worry about that most parents do not. How could we make her understand her brother's behaviour?

It is not easy for Jem having a brother like Jamie. Maybe if Jem was the older sibling she would see her brother as a vulnerable and sweet little person who needed her protection, but Jamie has always been a lot bigger and a lot stronger than her, so it is hard for her to see it that way.

It is also not easy for a parent to have to explain to a young child why she should forgive the person who has just spat at her, or broken her toys. I am not sure that there is actually a logical reason why she should.

Also, how do you apply different standards to different children? How do you explain to a child that she has to behave herself in a restaurant while her big brother is running around trying to grab pizzas from people's plates to use them as Frisbees?

If we get it wrong, Jem could grow up resenting her brother, and that would be one of the worst things I could think of.

I do not think that will happen though. Having Jamie as a brother has inhibited one or two aspects of Jem's life; we all have to work around his routine and his demands, and I know that that frustrates her. However we try to focus on some of the positive aspects, and make Jem see that having Jamie as a brother means that she gets to see life from a different angle to many of her friends.

Meg and I make such an effort to do fun things with her. We go out as a family of four as often as our nerves can handle it, and in addition, once a week we have a respite worker come to our house for a few hours to look after Jamie, so that Jem and Meg and I can go out and do something just the three of us.

Social services have helped, running "Young Carers" and "Siblings" groups for children in similar positions to Jem. They are a bit like youth clubs, doing fun things like parties, games and trips out. They provide a subtle form of counselling, but the thing I like most about them is the fact that it gives us something to point to, alongside not having to queue in theme parks, and say "This is all thanks to Jamie."

I am sure we make mistakes, all parents do. Maybe we are doing it all wrong. I hope not; but I want to be able to look back in ten years' time and say "we did our best".

I know that we are not a conventional family, but I think we manage to make it work. Just about.

The End

Epilogue

Jamie is now nearly a teenager.

He turned twelve recently, meaning that we have less than a year before he starts getting moody, experimenting with facial hair, locking himself in the bathroom for hours on end, and insisting on painting his room black.

Well, perhaps not, but who knows what his teenage years will bring? He is almost as tall as his mother now, and he is starting to fill out. Our biggest fear in recent years has been that he will become too big and too strong for us to control. We have given up with the medication, as it seems to make no difference.

Sometimes, when I talk to social workers or teachers, I see a look in their eyes that says "This guy has no idea what is about to hit him."

When Jamie is sixteen he will have to leave school. We have little idea what is going to happen to him then. It is certainly a cause for concern. I worry that the support available for disabled adults might not be as good as that available for disabled children. Also, Jamie's grandparents will be in their seventies by then, and not able to help out nearly as much.

And what about the more distant future? Will Jamie outlive his parents, and who will look after him then?

Our policy so far has been to take it a year at a time, and that policy has got us through the first twelve years, so we will carry on with it and worry in a few years' time about him leaving school.

Although we still have concerns for the future, I think that the fact that we have made it this far is reason for celebration, so I want to end this book on a positive note, and tell you about his twelfth birthday.

Jamie's twelfth birthday was a particularly joyous event. By coincidence, the birthday fell on the same day that my cousin Gary chose to get married to his lovely American girlfriend, Bailey. Meg, Jamie, Jemima and I made the long drive back up North. Jemima, as the flower girl, made a big impression during the day, but it was Jamie who stole the show in the evening. It was after the wedding breakfast and the speeches, while we were waiting for the disco to start, that we took Jamie away into a quiet side room, to give him his birthday cake and candles, and sing happy birthday to him.

We had wanted to make a bit of a fuss of him on his birthday, but we had wanted to do it quietly, without stealing any thunder from the bride and groom. We told a few close relatives what we were doing, and invited them to join us. However, it seems that each of these people told a few other people, and each of those told a few more, and so on. Within minutes, almost all of my side of the family were crammed into that small room. We started to sing Happy Birthday, and it quickly became apparent that they had all been drinking heavily, and that they were keen to show Jamie how fond they were of him by singing as loudly as they could. Let me tell you, drunken Geordies can sing very loudly indeed.

Jamie doesn't usually like being surrounded by people and noise, but for some reason this time, perhaps because he realised that it was all for him, he loved it. I have not seen him look as happy since *The Slipper Game*. The look of sheer delight on his face that evening was one that nobody who saw it will ever forget. I saw fully grown Geordie men with tears in their eyes as they were singing. I was one of them.

So that is where I wanted to end the story. I hope you have enjoyed this little book, and found it interesting here and there. I have enjoyed writing it.

"End" is the wrong word, perhaps. Our story is not really over. Our lives are still going on. I think it would be best to quit while we are ahead though, so I am going to stop writing now, before something else happens.

Acknowledgements

Most authors use this section to thank their editors, publishers, proof readers, and researchers. Well, I do not have any of those, so instead I will acknowledge the people who have helped over the years. In no particular order:

- Some great teachers at the Milestone School, Gloucester - especially Jayne English, Caroline Shaw, Bev Murray, and Kathleen Briggs. There were also loads of great classroom assistants, but I am not going to try to name them all in case I miss someone out.

- Jamie's respite carers Natasha Jones, Tom Askew, Caroline Shaw (again!) and Melanie Booth.

- The bus drivers and chaperones who have had to put up with so much over the years – especially Chris, Jan, Evita and Sharon.

- Debbie Nicholls, Jamie's extremely patient hairdresser.

- Kelsa Roland Evans, portage. She made it fun for both Jamie and Meg and was a good friend.

- Claire McGovern - Specialist Learning Disability Nurse. She has been amazing and Meg tells me that she might not have made it through the past few years without her.

- Diane, the excellent physiotherapist who coached Meg through the difficulties of the first year.

- We did not meet social worker Dave Wesson until after Jamie's twelfth birthday, so strictly speaking, I should wait until the sequel before thanking him. He has helped us a lot since then though, and I might never actually do a sequel (writing a book is hard you know, much harder than reading a book) so I will do it now instead. Thanks.

- Nick Jones, of "The Photo Studio", Tewkesbury. He took the photograph of Jamie that adorns the front cover. When I approached him recently to ask him for permission to use the picture, he remembered the photo-shoot even though it was almost ten years earlier, saying "Yes I remember, he is the little lad who liked switching plugs off!"

- Old friends and relatives – Mark Hutton, Gary Callan, Matt Pilcher, Claire Wedgebury, Martin and Caren, Mark and Vicky, Paul and Sarah, Caroline Howe, Suzanne, Andrew, Julian, Anna, Gary, Lesley, and Great Auntie Liz – all of whom made the effort to come and visit us or write to us during those difficult first few months. And also Jenny, who rang from Australia, and the girls from Meg's ward.

- Many of the parents of Jem's school friends who have helped us out in many ways over the years, especially Trish and Ian, and Tracey and Andy.
- My mother and father in law, who provided a lot of emotional support. Gordon also provided a lot of his DIY skills fixing the things that Jamie has broken / destroyed / kicked holes in over the years.
- My own mum and dad who have provided babysitting above and beyond the call of duty. We would have gone insane without them.
- Jamie's sister - Jemima, for saving us all.
- My wife Meg, who has been a wonderful wife and mother, and my best friend. She has worked so hard and been through so much to create a family home full of love, fun, and delicious cooking. Thank you.
- Finally, thanks to Jamie, without whom…well…you know.

Appendix

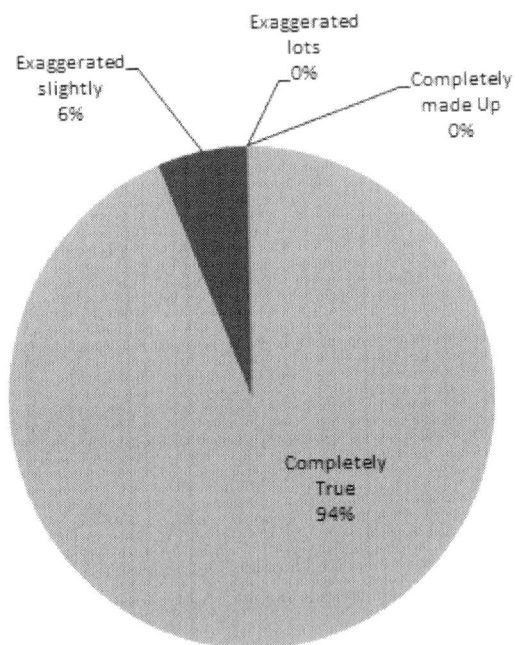

Truthfulness of Stories in Don't Let It Get You Down Syndrome

- Exaggerated slightly 6%
- Exaggerated lots 0%
- Completely made Up 0%
- Completely True 94%

26592297R00109

Printed in Great Britain
by Amazon